"Personal responsibility is the willingness to accept the consequences of one's behavior without blame or excuse. This quality is the bedrock of emotional stability and the lack of it is the financial cancer that almost destroyed the world financial markets in the first part of the twenty-first century. Mr. Kelly's book is a mirror for seeing what financial irresponsibility looks like. Whoever reads this book will see themselves as part of the problem instead of blaming everyone else. Like a happy movie ending, this book carefully explains what the average citizen can do to become financially responsible, worry free, and liberated from the bonds of the rich and powerful. If every American would read this book and follow its advice, America could be solvent and its citizens would have financial peace of mind. Get it now!"

—Terry Sandbek, Ph.D., Psychologist; Author, The *Worry Free Life*

"This book should be required reading in every high school economics class! Especially valuable is its clear explanation of how credit card debt works as compound interest in reverse. How lucky a young person would be to realize this before they fall into the bankster traps."

—Ralph Allswede, Retired President,
Precision Prototype & Mfg, Inc., and Consultant

"This is a most insightful and easy-to-read synopsis of the causes of our economic problems in the United States! The discussions about solutions are thought provoking. The writer has an easy to understand style that just keeps you reading till the pages run out!"

—C. Patrick Lauder, M.D., Mammoth Hospital, California

"One of my favorite books has been Piero Ferrucci's 'What We May Be,' a gem of transformational insight. On getting into Jason Kelly's abrasive depiction of financial incompetence, I was hardly thinking 'transformation.' Shocked resistance was the first reaction to his scolding against stupidity, claiming that America's most toxic asset is its financially stupid people. 'OMG, has the meticulously disciplined Jason of the 'Neatest Little Guide' series on investing, lost it, this time gambling that his rant against stupidity won't result in his readers thinking him a misanthrope?' Shock yielded to 'Aha' on feeling the hand of one who has made it, helping his readers along his well trodden path to economic character and a moral course to the good life. Kelly offers a rare and coherent fix on the interplay between societal economic chaos and the dysfunction of its individual members. The enemy is us, and the cure requires a resurgence of interest in individual character. "

—George Collins, Philosophy Professor, Attorney Estate Planner

"With disarming common sense, Kelly makes the case that personal financial freedom requires very little math skill. It depends mostly on our courage to question the social conventions built into modern consumption societies, and our resolve to change our lifestyles accordingly."

—Alan Furth, Economist; International Entrepreneur;
Blogger at AlanFurth.com

"In his latest book, Jason Kelly has given us a crash course in history and a review of the current state of our society and economy. He has shined a spotlight on the rampant lack of accountability that exists today and provided evidence that the cards are stacked against us. It's not all negative though, the book also provides a clear set of rules and tips for how to protect your wallet and get ahead. With real life examples of people from all walks of life, Jason illustrates that financial freedom is attainable for all of us."

—Jacob Glenn, Director Financial Services, Rosetta

"A must-read if the truth and reality of your financial future is important."

—Roger de Bock, Consultant, Western Financial Planning

Financially Stupid People are Everywhere

(with handwritten: STUPID)

are

Everywhere

Don't be one of them

Jason Kelly

WILEY

John Wiley & Sons, Inc.

For general information on our other products and services or for technical
support, please contact our Customer Care Department within the United States
at (800) 762-2974, outside the United States at (317) 572-3993 or
fax (317) 572-4002.

Wiley also publishes its books in a variety of electronic formats. Some content that
appears in print may not be available in electronic books. For more information
about Wiley products, visit our web site at www.wiley.com.

ISBN 978-0-470-57975-6

Printed in the United States of America

10 9 8 7 6 5 4 3 2 1

Contents

Contents

INTRODUCTION

Life as a Sucker

It's time we look honestly at what's really wrong with the American economy.

The whole thing nearly collapsed from overwhelming debt in a crisis that began in 2007 and is still raging as I write this in 2009. It seems the economy will survive for now, but thanks only to maniacal government spending—funded by taxpayers. The long-term consequences of that spending are probably dire, possibly catastrophic.

By most of the media's reckoning, the problem was that unscrupulous banks foisted bad loans on unsuspecting borrowers. Families were tricked into buying homes they couldn't afford, with mortgages they couldn't pay, based on incomes they didn't have. Because the banks bamboozled them, went the thinking, such people deserved to be bailed out. The mortgage payment plans *they agreed to follow* were restructured so they could stay in their homes. Both the bamboozling banks and the bamboozled people were bailed out with taxpayer dollars.

That's far from the whole story, though. The origins of the crisis extend much farther back than the bad mortgages of the early 2000s, to the creation of America's consumer culture of excess built on loose credit and mountains of debt. Responsibility became an endangered species, ravaged by ad-driven greed and instant gratification.

Washington justified its enormous bailouts. Banks that extended loans to people unable to repay were called too big to fail, and the people who borrowed their way into homes they couldn't afford were called victims.

For a moment, though, look closely at those victims, the supposedly poor people huddled in their supposedly humble shelters. The picture drawn by the popular story is of people in shabby clothes, sipping clear broth in a pool of candlelight for warmth, walking miles to a bus stop to go to a job that breaks their backs over the years. That's what hard times looked like to previous generations. It's not what we're talking about today.

Too many of today's "downtrodden" live in modern-day castles, wear designer clothes, drive opulent vehicles, eat in fine restaurants, take vacations, showcase "bling-bling" jewelry, and watch big-screen televisions. They fund their lifestyle with mortgages they can't afford and credit cards they don't understand. They live the life of Riley to show how sophisticated and cool they are, but when it all comes tumbling down they slink to Uncle Sam for help, not realizing that he's part of the problem. There's no dignity in that. It's shameful. Rather than whine for financial justice, they should hang their heads.

Banks got into trouble by lending money to such borrowers and then transforming the loans into exotic investments that skittered across the earth like locusts. The loans and securities based on them became known in the media as "toxic assets" that the government had to manage. Thing is, those assets didn't spring from nowhere. They were the prickly green weeds above ground, but they weren't the roots of the problem. The roots were the borrowers, those who signed on the line to a payment they couldn't afford. The borrowers, not the loans, were the problem.

Financially stupid people are America's most toxic asset.

They fail to see the money-trap society around them. They live in a world controlled by corporations seeking to extract as much of their wealth as possible, and the moronic masses open wide for every lure. They trust false promises of bought-off politicians. They sit mesmerized before advertising campaigns telling them to buy trifles they don't need using debt they can't repay. They stumble down the path paved by big business that transfers their income to corporate coffers. They don't realize that the way of the world is not the way they want to live, then they wonder what happened when they end up broke and hopeless. What happened is that they fell for the pattern, the easy route, the stairway to serfdom. They did not take control of their own financial future. They did not guard their wealth-building effort against the flim-flammery of a debt-based culture concocted by corporate boardrooms and made into law by puppeteered politicians.

Do companies try to trick people? Of course they do, and always have.

Take credit cards, for example. All you need to know about the credit card industry is that it couldn't exist if everybody paid on time. Profits come from people carrying balances at obscene interest rates. The smart people who pay off their cards every month get an interest-free loan. The morons who pay the minimum each month enter indentured servitude where every price becomes a multiple of its original value.

Wake up, America!

Yes, they're trying to trick you, but if you're not a moron and figure out the system, the joke's on them. They'll send you enticing checks drawn on your credit card and tell you to show yourself a good time. They'll affix advertisements to your payment slip to try to get you to spend more money even as you pay on what you already spent. They'll print in bold type the minimum amount you need to pay this month, not the balance in full. But if you laugh at their little tricks and pay off the full balance through it all, you win and they lose. It's their own fault for creating a system based on the principle of providing enough rope for people to hang themselves. If you use the rope for something other than tying a noose around your neck, it's a good free rope. If you use a credit card for something other than debt accumulation, it's a good free loan month after month on the bank's dime.

Society's trap is this simple: You're made to want what you don't need, then provided with debt to get it. When you dive down the debt hole, you can't easily get out so they've got you right where they want you, paying interest forever, stuck at a job you probably don't like, generating taxes that politicians transform into profits for their big business benefactors. Bought the wrong way, houses, cars, and all manner of trifles lead to that grim existence.

The only reason America wound up on a mountain of teetering debt is that financially stupid people piled it up. The banks offered—and they're a bunch of bastards, it's true—but it's the borrowers who accepted. People who accept debt are suckers. Instead of being a sucker, wouldn't you like to look across the desk at that scheming banker or blustering businessman and laugh as you turn down every gimmick he offers? Wouldn't you like to know he never got a single dime of damaging interest out of you, and will never lay hands on your financial freedom? I would, I do, and you can, too. We all can. That's the point of this book.

When you finish reading, you'll see how to buck the debt trend by following the First Rule of Finance and controlling the Three Cs. You'll understand the pervasiveness of the enemy around you, the government, bank, and big-business faction that engineered ways to get your wealth before you were even born. You'll understand that almost all of society's decisions are made financially, and that you need to think financially as well in order to grow your wealth. You'll employ a simple system for marching up the net worth slope against a gale force wind of special interests trying to slow you down.

Introduction: Life as a Sucker

Financial people are everywhere in society's leadership positions, pulling levers to make every option in front of citizens hazardous to their wealth. Financial*ly stupid* people are everywhere among the population, failing to grasp what's really going on and repeatedly making choices that benefit the schemers. Don't be one of the financially stupid. See through the haze. Guard your future. Refuse society's claim on your financial freedom.

The nature of your whole life comes down to how you answer one question: Will I live in debt or will I live free?

This book will make sure you live free.

CHAPTER 1

The First Rule of Finance

The First Rule of Finance is to live within your means by spending no more than 80 percent of your take-home pay.

If you take home $100 per week, spend no more than $80. If you take home $1,000 per week, spend no more than $800. If you take home $10,000 per week, spend no more than $8,000 or, better yet, keep living as you did back when you made only $1,000 per week, because that's enough.

From this simple rule, all else falls into place. If you don't spend more than 80 percent of your income, you won't get into trouble. You won't allow house payments, car payments, insurance payments, and shopping charges to exceed your 80 percent threshold. You may not be Einstein, but you can manage this concept, right?

That's all we're talking about here. When you read that people were tricked by mean bankers, remember the First Rule of Finance and ask how anybody can be tricked into spending more than 80 percent of their income. How stupid are they?

Prove to yourself that humanity is up to the task of adding and subtracting. Test a son, daughter, nephew, niece, or neighbor kid. Give them ten bucks and tell them they can

7

buy anything they want with it, but you want at least two dollars back then they're done. Drive them to a store and watch the magic. They look at prices, they look at their ten bucks, if they're really sharp they account for sales tax, and they find something for less than eight dollars. Bingo! A financial wizard is born.

It's really that simple.

Wealth springs from this First Rule of Finance. That's why it's first. Troubles begin the moment it's broken. The day you commit to spending less than 80 percent of your income is the day you start getting rich.

Killing Themselves for the Joneses

Ever look at what people spend their money on? I have relatives and friends chronically in debt, spending $12 for every $10 they earn instead of the $8 you know they should be spending. When I see them, they're proud of their new whatever. Cars are high on the list. Electronics, too. A few boats have shown up. Designer clothing is popular. "What do you think of my new truck?" asked one from the driver's seat. "Do you like my new shoes?" asked another on stiletto heels. "Check out my new big screen," said a third while holding the remote in his living room. We've all heard people fishing for compliments on their new toys.

Theirs?

The first guy didn't own the truck, the bank did—and eventually repossessed it. The woman didn't own the shoes, she made payments on them to the bank issuing one of her many credit cards and still pays on them today even though they've long since gone out of style. What did she do? Replaced them with new ones, of course—before she'd ever paid off the old ones. The third person didn't own the big-screen TV, he financed it with in-store credit that came interest-free for 90 days, then hit him with all the backed-up interest plus penalties if he was late in paying, which, of course, he was. These people don't own anything.

Every one of them was proud of what they'd financed. They seem to have bought it for the purpose of being proud, of showing off, of keeping up with the Joneses. Nice cars beget nicer cars, nice shoes beget nicer shoes, and big TVs beget bigger TVs. "Look at my new . . ." is everybody's favorite phrase, even when the object in question isn't theirs at all and won't be new when they've finally paid for it, if they ever do.

They're proud of being stupid. They think it's cool to drive the financed car, wear the financed shoes, and watch the financed TV, but to smart people, whose opinions are the only ones we should respect, these people look dumb as rocks.

The Joneses Are Broke

The following is an *Investopedia* article on conspicuous consumption, by Lisa Smith:

> It used to be that spending money on status symbols for the sake of flaunting your wealth was an activity reserved for celebrities and millionaires. That has all changed. Conspicuous consumption, what was once referred to as "keeping up with the Joneses," has brought the lifestyles of the rich and famous to suburbia.
>
> Just as most people consider themselves to be above-average drivers, most people assume they aren't the ones doing all this needless spending. They aren't wearing ten pounds of gold chains or gowns created by famous designers. Four-hundred-dollar haircuts, sprawling mansions, Rolls-Royces, and private planes aren't in their budget, so they assume their spending is reasonable. However, a closer look at what you're spending might put your own lifestyle in a different light. . . .
>
> *(continued)*

(continued)

Many of the people driving around the suburbs in their giant SUVs while talking on their new cell phones are deeply in debt. If you ask them how they are doing, they will tell you that they are just barely getting by. According to a Federal Reserve Board study, 43 percent of American families spend more than they earn.

Source: Lisa Smith, "Stop Keeping Up With The Joneses—They're Broke," *Investopedia,* http://www.investopedia.com/articles/pf/07/conspicuous_consumption.asp.

The Joneses, nine times out of ten, are financially stupid. That's why they have all that stuff, on borrowed money. Why try to copy them? Worse, why try to impress them? Copy and impress smart people, the ones who own their stuff. If you want to impress smart people, debt is the last way to go about it. Trying to impress a money-smart person by going into debt is like trying to impress Olympic swimming champion Michael Phelps by drowning in a pool, or golf pro Tiger Woods by driving your ball through the windshield of a parked car. Michael Phelps is impressed by good swimming, Tiger Woods by good golfing, and a money-smart person by good money management.

First Save, Then Buy

If you ever want to know how predictably stupid most people are and how smart people are onto them, attend a product-and-marketing meeting. Companies that make and sell shiny objects know what they're doing, and they consider the average consumer to be a complete dope. I once joined a meeting at an electronics manufacturer where a manager asked if people would really buy a big-screen TV model as big and expensive as the one discussed that day. "Sure," said an executive, "just show a celebrity using it and break the price into 60 monthly payments that don't begin for six months, and they'll buy anything." Everybody laughed and nodded, because he was right. The same meetings happen at car companies, clothing companies, furniture companies, and jewelry companies. Most consumers are just walking debt dopes. Companies know that and have learned the language and images that trick the dopes into piling on more debt.

"I deserve this," says one debt dope.

"It fits my lifestyle," says another.

"In today's world, your car is your home away from home," regurgitates a third.

O First Rule of Finance, First Rule of Finance! Where art thou, First Rule of Finance?

Here's a little secret: most of the joy of buying is anticipation. Dreaming and saving for the car of your dreams is the best part. Once you buy it, it's just your car. Same with a pair of designer stilettos. Same with a big-screen TV. Life is long. When you buy everything you want immediately, there's nothing to look forward to anymore.

Instead, get your life on the First Rule of Finance, save a foundation of money, and make purchases from it. If you see a big-screen TV you want that costs $5,000, break it down into 24 monthly payments of $210 into your own savings account *before you buy*, and enjoy counting the months and watching the cash pile up. On top of the joy you'll get anticipating the day you walk in and slap cash on the counter, four fringe benefits will emerge:

1. The money you save will generate interest until the day you use it. Keep that for yourself instead of paying it to bankers and corporate tycoons. You'll read later how the Federal Reserve sometimes destroys this benefit by lowering interest rates to encourage spending, but for now just know that saving puts whatever interest is available into *your* pocket, instead of a corporation's.

2. By the time you've saved enough for the object of your desire, there will probably be a newer and better model available for the same price or less.
3. You will own free and clear the object in its most pristine state when it's brand spanking new. Debt dopes never own anything, or by the time they do own things they're old and in need of replacement—with further debt.
4. You will never suffer buyer's remorse because your purchases will be carefully planned. You won't jump into anything lame and then suffer paying it off for years.

First save, then buy.

By saving and then buying, you pace your purchases, enjoy them much more, and never get into debt. Most people do just the opposite. They buy everything they want the moment they see it, rack up a mountain of debt, and add to the mountain when they buy new things.

That's the debt cycle, and the economy is built on it. During the credit crisis, the government said repeatedly that it needed to get banks lending again and people shopping again, even though it was excessive borrowing and shopping that created the crisis. "Holy smokes!" Washington exclaimed. "We have to *stimulate* banks into lending so people and businesses borrow and spend, so we can get right back to the debt-based economy that got us into this mess. Hurry!"

At the time, I remarked to my smart friends that if everybody lived the way we do, there could be no debt economy. Companies can't force us to buy things. Buying is voluntary. If people restricted themselves to buying what they could pay for with cash, companies would adjust by offering only reasonably priced goods. Companies will never stop making shiny objects that are too expensive as long as debt dopes line up to buy them on credit. If enough people wise up, though, companies will change their ways and surround us with affordable goods.

CHAPTER 2

Credit, Cars, and Castles

The serial killers of financial lives are credit, cars, and castles. Almost every debt disaster on two feet began among the Three Cs. Credit card debt is some of the most expensive on Earth, topped only by cash from Tony Soprano. New cars have been too expensive for decades, but continue being offered at obscene prices because stupid people fall for financing programs. Castles are our homes, and despite their ability to boost net worth by appreciating, stupid people found a way to screw them up, too. Let's look at all Three Cs.

Credit Cards

If I were named America's financial czar for a day, I would outlaw credit cards. A collective outcry would blast from banks and idiots, but then people would adjust. Under the Kelly regime, the only legal plastic spending would happen on debit cards limited to the balance in the buyer's account. People would carry those or, here's an idea, carry cash. Either way, they'd spend only what they have. Within a few years it would be the norm.

It's already the norm in Japan. When people from the countryside go on day trips to Tokyo, how much cash do you think they carry? No, not $10. No, not $100. They take somewhere between $500 and $1,000. It helps that there are no criminals, of course, but that's the subject of a different manifesto.

I've seen people in Japan pay for five-course dinners with cash, new wardrobes with cash, new cars with cash, and a $30,000 funeral with cash. Many restaurants and stores in Japan don't even accept credit cards. "Why would I?" one store owner asked me. "I'd have to pay a fee, and it's bad for customers." Indeed!

You've heard the knee-jerk defenses of credit cards: they're convenient, they provide a back-up in case of emergencies, they're safer than cash in cases of theft or loss. All true, but debit cards provide those same benefits without any danger of debt. With credit cards, all of those benefits are overwhelmingly outweighed by the financial damage that credit card debt has caused. Like the toxic assets of bad loans in the credit crisis, though, the cards themselves are not the root problem. The idiots carrying them are. So, let's focus on the idiots, *again*. Don't you get tired of them?

Here's quick proof that most people are financial imbeciles: Only improperly used credit cards are profitable to their issuing banks. The banks keep issuing cards, though, so you know the majority of people use their cards improperly. Improperly means carrying a balance and paying interest and late fees.

Credit-card industry revenue breaks down like this: 80 percent from interest payments and late fees, 20 percent in fees paid by merchants who accept the cards. If people smartened up, the 80 percent would go to zero and the 20 percent would probably drop dramatically because overall use of cards would decline as people stopped needing debt. Former card-swipers would see that, since they pay their balance off each month anyway, they might as well pay cash and avoid the whole billing hassle. That's why I claim that if everybody used their credit cards properly, the industry would disappear.

If you pay off the balance on a no-fee credit card every month, the joke's on the issuing bank. They're giving you a free loan while hoping with their greedy stone hearts that you slip up some time or, even better, repeatedly . . . forever. It's so much fun to never slip up, though, and giggle each time they print the minimum payment bigger, or try to hide the balance in fine print, or send a letter encouraging you to use the card in new ways for "the lifestyle you deserve," or offer an incentive interest rate on balance transfers. "Balance?" smart people say. "Oh, no, no, no, my little banking demon friend. I *never* carry a balance, so there's nothing to transfer, and I couldn't care less what interest rate you're offering because it *never* affects me. So go to hell."

To financially smart people, credit cards pose no danger. To the really smart, they provide an easy way to use the bank to one's advantage for a change.

Here's one of my all-time favorite credit-card stories. Years ago, I self-published a book. It sold well, and I went back to the printer several times for more copies. Each time, I needed to pay the printer immediately for the work, and then sell the books. I paid expenses before receiving income, so cash flow was tricky to manage. If I wasn't careful, I could run out of cash during the time between paying for books and receiving income for their sales. The printer would not grant my small company a line of credit. What to do?

Turn to my credit card. It was already a line of credit, after all, and if I timed the big printing charges correctly, I could get up to two months of interest-free money. How did that work? The end of the billing cycle happened on the 20th of each month. I told the printer to charge the entire cost on the 21st. The next credit card statement wouldn't be mailed until the following month and wouldn't be due for payment until the month after that. Ta da! Two months of interest-free money. That was enough time to capture cash flow from selling the books, so I'd be able to pay the printer charges in full when the credit-card bill came due.

That, right there, is enough to make this a good story, but here's what makes it a great story. My card rewarded me with free gasoline at a national chain, based on a percentage of what I spent on the card. That's what incentive programs are supposed to do, encourage people to spend. The programs work for the issuing bank because the bank knows most people are financial dolts and will end up carrying their balance forward, in the process incurring interest and fees that *greatly* exceed the value of the incentive program. My card gave 1 percent of all purchases back as free gasoline credits, and 5 percent of purchases made at that chain of gas stations. My printing charges came to $10,000 or $20,000 each time. At a rate of 1 percent, I would get back $100 or $200 worth of free gasoline every time I printed more books.

I got my books printed, paid the printer immediately on the card, sold the books, paid the full balance on the card two months after printing, never paid a dime of interest, and built up a ton of gasoline credits. I enjoyed free fill-ups for more than a year because of that. Who paid for them? The bank, but you know who really paid? All the stupid people carrying balances on their cards. Thanks to their financial witlessness, the bank makes enough profit off the card program to be able to offer free gasoline to all card holders. The dopes revel in every $1 of free gasoline they receive while paying 18 percent interest on the $100 they spent to get it. Basic math, people. Basic math.

In a sense, we smarties should be grateful for the dummies because their mistakes help us get ahead. I'd rather see a country filled with financially stable households, though. I'd pay for my own gasoline in exchange for that.

The simple rule for credit cards is this: Never carry a balance.

Is that so hard? Of course not, and especially not if you're already following the First Rule of Finance. Limiting your spending to 80 percent of your take-home pay automatically keeps you from going nuts with a credit card.

If you can't follow the never-carry-a-balance rule, then at least be smart enough to cut up your credit cards and replace them with a debit card. Notice, a *single* debit card. An overabundance of plastic casts immediate suspicion on a person's financial intelligence, and *Newsweek* reported in 2008 that the typical American household held 13 credit cards, so you know it's a nation of nincompoops. There's no reason to carry a wallet or purse filled with multiple credit and debit cards. If you have your act together, you need just one. If it's a credit card, you make the month's purchases on it, then pay it off. You'll never max it out and need to use another one. Leave that humiliation to the debt dopes. You either pay your credit card in full each month so the balance is never in danger of maxing out, or use a debit card that is good for the full cash balance of your bank account.

And, here's a thought. If you ever max out, *stop buying things.* That's an option.

This stuff isn't hard. Anybody can do it, and we need to stop feeling sorry for those who are "in over their heads" because they couldn't understand four stinkin' words: Never carry a balance.

Cars

Right after credit cards, automobiles rank as the most dangerous liability in America. Notice, not *asset*, but *liability.* Few people own their cars. Most people's cars own them. Automobiles begin depreciating the moment you buy them, and cost a fortune at face value and a double fortune when financed. Naturally, because the country is filled with financial fools, most people finance.

Automotive financing is the reason shaved-headed punks can drive $40,000 SUVs in Los Angeles. One day, I grew so fed up with seeing that, I approached a punk in a parking garage where he hung out with friends in front of a new black SUV with chrome hubs and tinted windows and a pounding stereo.

"Nice ride," I said.

"Thanks, man," he replied, and he and all his friends nodded and gawked at the SUV.

"When will you own it?" I asked.

"Whaddaya mean? I already bought it."

"Really? That must have set you back. How long did it take you to save that kind of cash?"

"No, I didn't have to pay cash. I make a payment every month." He looked at me like I was crazy. Hello? Doesn't everybody make payments?

"Oh, so then you don't actually own it yet. When will you own it?"

"I don't know, seven years or something," he said.

"I wonder if it'll still be cool when you finally own it?"

I then walked away to the sweet sound of insults. I checked the price of that SUV at a dealership. Sure enough, $40 grand. That was pre-bling. He probably added another $2,000 in hubs and rims and whatnot. When you're spending funny money anyway, why stop?

So, how much do you think the cool cat in L.A. paid for his ride? If we take his "seven years or something" to mean seven years (Can you imagine not even knowing the length of the loan?) and the interest rate was 10 percent, Boy Genius ended up paying $55,776. That's a $664 payment for 84 months.

The curious thing is, if he and I went together to the dealership and he jumped up and down and pointed at the SUV screaming "gimme, gimme, gimme!" and I said only after he saved $664 per month for the next 84 months, he'd have thrown a tantrum. "I only make $2,000 a month," he'd have said. "So how can I possibly save that much?"

Righty-o, tough guy, which is why it's the wrong vehicle for you.

By the way, we're not even done with how much the SUV actually cost. On top of the $664 monthly tally, he had to pay insurance and registration. Insurance would have cost at least $100 per month and California would have added $3,600 to the initial cost of the vehicle.

If people needed to pay cash for cars, how many models do you think would sell for more than $10,000? Very few. Saving $300 per month for three years creates $10,800. That should be enough to get a decent car, but people's idea of a decent car has been warped by years of advertising, and car companies have succeeded in convincing the financially brain-dead that every car should be bought with financing.

It need not be so.

For starters, there are plenty of good used cars available. Let nitwits like Boy Genius in L.A. pick up the depreciation tab. He's dumb enough to want a brand-new SUV within a year or two, well before his "seven years or something" are up, and he'll then trade in the one I saw for a new one. If you want an SUV like his, just wait for his attention span to expire. He will have suffered the damage of the steepest part of the depreciation curve, after which you show up. He's off to another financial disaster, you're off in a fairly new and still very cool vehicle at a fraction of its sticker price.

I sometimes lurk in dealer showrooms to overhear the accidents in progress. These occur more often in showrooms than on the road. Salespeople say things like "fits your lifestyle" and "matches your image." The most common debt-dope comment, heard before he or she signs the dotted line into servitude, is "I deserve this."

Says who? Deserve is an odd duck. What's it based on? Who decides what adds up to deserving anything? If we remove the ability to pay from the definition, then it's just a feeling. You know how to know when you deserve a certain car? When you set your sights on it, save carefully for it, and show the discipline to gather enough cash to buy it. Then, and only then, can you walk into a dealership and point to the car of your dreams and say proudly that you deserve it. Before that day, you're just another debt accumulator.

The simple rule for buying an automobile is this: Don't finance.

Pretty straightforward, isn't it? That one idea will automatically force you to think carefully about the kind of car you really need. If you decide that you want a whopper like that $40,000 SUV, then you're going to have to work really hard at your job or business to save the cash needed to make it happen—and that's how it should be. The process will build in you a deep love of that vehicle you want so badly. The steady saving of cash will build in you an appreciation of the value of money. Each $100 you sock away will represent a number of bricks delivered, or shelves stocked, or children taught, or engines fixed, or juries addressed, or fields plowed, or eyes checked, or whatever it is you do. If you still want the dream car after you've saved enough to buy it, that will be a day circled forever on your calendar as the day you stood proud and paid cash for what you dreamed about for years.

Before that day, you'll need to get around in a car that's not the one of your dreams. So what? Sam Walton of Wal-Mart drove an old truck even *after* he became a billionaire. Warren Buffett drives a 2001 Lincoln Town Car with a license plate that reads THRIFTY. Microsoft cofounder Paul Allen drives a 1988 Mazda B-Series pickup. If anybody deserves fancy cars, it's these billionaires, but look at what's good enough for them. Rather than trying to keep up with the Jones jerks and their chain debt habit, keep up with the billionaires and the affordable cars they own. Not *finance*, mind you; *own*.

The best way to avoid finance charges and keep taxes, registration, insurance, and maintenance costs low is to pay cash for cars that are two or three years old.

When you're starting out, you may find yourself in a pinch where you need to finance in order to get a reliable first car. If so, do it reluctantly and promise yourself that you're breaking the rule for just a short time until you pay off that car, then keep driving it fully paid while you save up enough cash so that you never need finance again. The bozo habit to avoid is making payments on one car right up until you buy another car, then making payments on that one until you buy another one, and so on, until decades go by and you've lost thousands of dollars by making a rip-off car payment every month of your life. Don't be a bozo!

How about a rule for breaking the rule? If you *must* finance your first car for reasons I don't even want to hear—undoubtedly taken from the latest car commercial canard about safety, because everybody feels good about that—at least keep the payment under 10 percent of your take-home pay. If you take home $3,000 per month, spend no more than $300 on a car payment, and do it for just three years. At a 10 percent interest rate, that'll get you into a $9,300 car, a price that includes many fine models made in the last few years.

I can't emphasize enough that this is not an excuse for you to blow 10 percent of your take-home pay toward a car for the rest of your life. It's just a stopgap measure for people in a pinch, and should not last longer than a single three-year period. No exceptions. Financial pinches that last longer than three years are not pinches, they're permanent bad habits, and are precisely what we're trying to avoid here.

Conserve Car Cash

It never hurts to save a few bucks on the car you already own. Here are some tips to keep expenditures down.

Skip the premium gas. Buy the cheapest gasoline that doesn't cause your engine to knock. The only benefit of higher octane is the absence of knocking, so pay as little as possible for that benefit.

Don't automatically change your oil every 3,000 miles. Check your car's manual to see what the manufacturer suggests. Newer cars can often go 5,000 or even 7,500 miles between oil changes.

(continued)

(continued)

As long as you have the manual out, go by the factory's maintenance schedule instead of a dealer's. Any dealer wants to see your car as much as possible, and you'll pay dearly for the visits.

Speaking of dealers, avoid them if you can. Find a reliable independent mechanic in your area, get to know him on a first-name basis, give him a birthday card every year, and you'll save thousands. For peace of mind, be sure he's certified by the National Institute for Automotive Service Excellence.

There are at least a few things you should do yourself, even if you're no mechanic: replace your windshield wipers, replace your air filter after every other oil change, and keep your tires properly inflated with a monthly pressure check. Improperly inflated tires waste gasoline, wear out more quickly, and blow out more often.

As for me, I've never owned a new car and probably never will. You know why? Because years ago on a lark I collected car commercials from two years prior to see how they compared to new commercials. The new commercials emphasized engine performance and safety features, and showed sparkly cars driving on country roads and through cityscapes. What do you think commercials from two years prior emphasized? Yep, engine performance and safety features, along with shots of cars on country roads and in cityscapes. Vehicles just don't change that much from year to year. They've provided perfectly fine performance and a slew of excellent safety features for more than a decade. The last big automotive safety leap was the airbag, and it was patented in the early 1970s. It hit the broad market in the 1980s, then dual airbags and side airbags became popular in the 1990s. Cars made two years ago are almost exactly as safe as cars made today. There's little reason to pay more for this year's model. If you want to feel good about a two-year-old model, go back and look at its commercials. They'll make you want to buy it as much as new commercials make you want to buy the new model—but you'll get a huge discount on the pre-owned vehicle. That's why recent models are good enough for me. If I want this year's, I'll get it two years from now—and enjoy the wait. I'll also enjoy the savings. Two-year-old models are 20 to 40 percent cheaper than new models.

You may feel more passionate about cars, though, and maybe you dream of a brand new model. That's fine. As long as you save and pay cash for it, you won't go wrong.

Castles

You need somewhere to live. It's going to cost money whether you buy or rent. Despite all you've read about home ownership being the American dream, renting often makes sense. Home ownership involves costs and headaches that might not be worth the tax benefits and investment benefits it brings. So, right up front, I want you to know I don't think you're a diminished American if you choose to rent instead of buy. I rented at times in my life, and they were good times.

Why might renting be better for you than buying? You're freer, for starters. It's a lot easier to pack up and move somewhere when you rent. You don't have any maintenance duties or expenses, which are a big deal for people like me who don't like fixing things and mowing lawns. Also, you might get more home for your money by renting. When you're young, for instance, you'll have a hard time affording a home with a swimming pool, but some apartments include one.

If you decide to rent, spend no more than a fifth of your take-home pay, which is a quarter of your 80 percent spending limit. (Remember the First Rule of Finance?) If you take home $2,500 per month, your spending limit is $2,000 and a quarter of that is $500. Find a $500 apartment. If you take home $5,000 per month, your spending limit is $4,000 and a quarter of that is $1,000. Find a $1,000 apartment. If you take home $500 per month, find a better job.

If you decide to buy a house, set your heart on an actual house, not a modern-day castle. Way too many new houses are way too big, which makes them way too expensive to buy, heat, and cool. Of course, way too many people buy just such monstrosities because they think they'll impress the Joneses, who are idiots. Be clear that you'll buy a house for your family, not a castle for the Joneses.

Once you've established that, save enough to make at least a 20 percent down payment. I don't care if a double-dealing bank says you can move in without a down payment. They're not doing you a favor. They do themselves favors, not you, so any favors on your end are going to have to come from you. Do yourself one by making a 20 percent down payment.

It helps you in two ways.

First, it gives you an immediate ownership stake in the place and is something you can be proud of. Remember pride? It used to blaze down on America like light from the sun. Now it comes in occasional rays through an overcast sky, but it's still there. Grab a little for yourself by saving the money needed to *buy* your home, not just move in. A 20 percent down payment shows you're serious, and responsible, and proud. An adult!

Second, a 20 percent down payment gets around private mortgage insurance, or PMI. If you put down less than 20 percent, careful lenders think you present a high risk of default and demand PMI to cover that risk. A 20 percent down payment gives them cash to cover risk, and also demonstrates that you have your financial act together and are probably a good bet. If you haven't even been able to scrape together a down payment, how good will you be at making monthly payments? It's a fair question, and one a proud home-buyer avoids by putting 20 percent down.

So then, 20 percent of how much? Try to get your total monthly payment—called PITI for principal, interest, (property) taxes, and insurance—to fall somewhere between 30 and 40 percent of your monthly take-home pay. You're already used to keeping your housing payment at 20 percent from when you rented, now let's add on another 10 for home ownership to get 30 percent, the low end of the range. If you take home $5,000 per month, you can afford a $1,500 mortgage payment. At 6 percent annual interest for 30 years, that'll cover a $250,000 loan. Not bad. You could either make a $50,000 down payment on that to get the loan to $200,000 for a lower monthly payment, or make a 20 percent down payment on a place that costs as much as $312,500 to get the $250,000 mortgage. Follow that? Just in case: 20 percent of $312,500 is a down payment of $62,500. Subtract that from $312,500 and you're left with a $250,000 mortgage that requires a $1,500 monthly payment. On top of that you'll pay property taxes and insurance for another $100 or $200. You can run different numbers at bankrate .com, mortgage-calc.com, and other sites.

Notice that you're still well within the First Rule of Finance. You take home $5,000 per month, can spend up to $4,000 of it, but have spent only $1,700 or so on your home. That leaves another $2,300 for everything else in life, like food, fashion, fuel, and fun.

You probably think the down payment is big. It is, but shouldn't it be? You're buying a house, after all, and houses are about the biggest purchases you can make. Thanks to your adhering to the First Rule of Finance, you'll be able to save the down payment in a reasonable amount of time. In the above examples, you needed to save $50,000 or $62,500. Say you start your first real job at age 22 after college, and you take home $2,500 per month. You're spending just 80 percent of that, so the extra 20 percent puts $500 into your savings every month. That's $6,000 per year. Even without raises or bonuses, by the time you're 30 you'll have saved $48,000 for a down payment. Excellent work! Who cares about owning a home when they're in their 20s, anyway? When you consider the likelihood of earning more money as you get older and better at what you do, and the chances of meeting a significant other to contribute toward financial progress, the odds of your being able to responsibly buy a home in your 30s are high. That's if you want to. Remember, renting is also a valid option.

The simple rule for buying a house is this: Put 20 percent down, and keep the mortgage payment below 40 percent of your take-home pay.

Kinda makes you wonder about all those people who fell for the shiny hook of a subprime loan, doesn't it? No money down? Bad sign. Teaser rate? Bad sign. So-called "no-doc" home loan, as in "no documentation of any kind whatsoever required"? Bad sign. What kind of financial numbskull really thinks a purchase as big as a home should happen with no paperwork? One shady no-doc vendor advertised, "No Income, No Tax Returns, No W2s, No Job, Nothing!" Again, we come back to the issue of pride. Do you really want to be part of that miserable crowd? Of course not. You're better than that. You're in a better country than that. You work for your money, you contribute to society, you're good for the loan, and you're buying a home the right way—or not at all.

Toxic FSP in the Alphabet of Idiocy

Now you know how people *should* manage their finances. Most come nowhere near it, however. Instead of never carrying a balance on credit cards, they always carry a balance. Instead of paying cash for a car they can afford, they become chain borrowers, taking on new car debt before paying off old car debt. Instead of putting 20 percent down on a house they can afford, they put down as little as possible on the biggest house they can get away with. When their fraudulent finances don't work out, they complain that the system is stacked against them. "It's unfair," they cry. "I can't get ahead. Nobody's looking out for me!"

Never have we heard that cry more shrilly than after the housing market went bust in 2006, debt dopes "in over their heads" stopped making payments on the mortgage contracts they'd signed, the mortgages held as bonds and equities blew up banks and investors over the next two years, the economy swirled dangerously close to the bottom of the toilet bowl in 2008 and 2009, and the government rushed in with trillions of taxpayer dollars to "save the system" from total collapse. Among the many measures taken, government provided "stimulus," intended to get banks lending again. That was the first order of the day. God knows we wouldn't want to end up with an economy based on something other than debt.

In all the talk of economic meltdown, the media blamed the Federal Reserve for putting too much money on the street, blamed mortgage brokers for lending it out at easy terms, blamed banks for going along with the loans that came in from the brokers, blamed financiers for inventing ways to repackage and resell those loans, blamed home-builders for building more houses than the market could support, blamed housing prices for falling instead of rising forever, and blamed corporations for laying people off when the economy stalled.

Nobody blamed the borrowers.

Keep that in mind as we take a quick look back at what went wrong.

What Went Wrong

After the dot-com bubble burst in the year 2000, the Federal Reserve cut interest rates repeatedly to protect the economy and Wall Street from plummeting tech-stock prices. That's called opening the taps and blasting the market with "liquidity," which is what investors call money. Lower interest rates make money cheap, and cheap money flooded America in the early 2000s. Where did it go? The housing market. Banks wanted to lend it out, of course. That's their business. They targeted home loans, and we were off to the races. Bigger, easier loans attracted more people to the housing market, their demand sent prices soaring, and it became a free-for-all on Main Street.

To the ten or so people smart enough to notice that housing prices were too high for them to afford, this posed no problem. Too high to afford meant "don't buy." To millions of morons, however, it meant "borrow more." America's consumer culture of excess kicked in. *Too much is never enough.*

You can have it all. Take it to the limit. Those sentiments were beaten into brains by decades of advertising and made possible by loose credit. The culture spawned a number of societal problems, both nonfinancial and financial alike. The same mind-set that encourages you to "supersize" your meal when you're hungry and just buy bigger clothing when you're fat, also encourages you to supersize the home you want to buy and just borrow more money when you can't afford it. Reasonable price? That is *so* three-generations-ago.

Lenders fanned the flames of deluded desire with longer terms, low down payments, and then no down payments, adding on teaser rates that stayed artificially low for a couple of years before resetting to a higher rate. The excitement grew. There was no end to this party! Rising excitement, rising demand, rising prices, rising stakes—remind you of anywhere? How about Atlantic City, Macau, Monte Carlo, and Las Vegas? The U.S. housing market became a giant casino, and in every casino, most people lose. This one would prove no different.

Sound banking practices that include quaint steps like checking a borrower's ability to repay, flew out the window. Greed overwhelmed common sense, and banks decided they needed more business than even the surging demand could provide. Why wait for a rube to walk in the door asking for a loan when one could be actively solicited? Thus entered mortgage brokers, middlemen who didn't actually provide the money or service the loan, but just found dopes to sign mortgage agreements, and then sold those mortgages to whichever banks would buy them. The broker faced no liability once the dope, er, client, was tossed over the wall to the bank. They collected their fee for having sourced the business and signed up the rube, then they were off in search of another brainless hand holding a signing pen.

This was pure heaven to greedy bankers and brokers. As the brokers chewed their way through qualified buyers, then less qualified, then questionable, then unqualified, then unemployed, then to anybody who could hold a pen, the quality of mortgages steadily fell. Big surprise, eh? That's where the term subprime came in. Had the loans made to people lower on the lending food chain been called deadbeat debt or time bomb banking, they may have proved less popular. But they were inoffensively called subprime, so even rubes felt good signing on.

Rising home prices created an illusion of wealth, which the non-thinking immediately turned into even more debt by taking out second mortgages and home equity lines of credit. They owned little or none of their home to begin with, but then set off to add more debt to their already staggering sum. For that second (or third, or fourth) round of borrowing against a home, there is almost no excuse. The borrowed money doesn't buy the home, so nobody can point to that reason. Technically, a person could use the proceeds of a second mortgage for something productive like a home improvement that would boost the value of the home, or another investment that would end up being worth more than the amount borrowed with interest, but almost nobody did anything smart like that. If they had, their financial situations would have improved and we wouldn't have had a crisis. Instead, they treated their homes like ATMs to borrow cash and go shopping for trifles. A home is not an ATM, though. At least when people take cash from an ATM, it's cash that is truly theirs. When they borrow cash against the value of a home they don't yet own, they sink farther into the quicksand of debt and have even higher interest expenses to shoulder.

An odd thing happens when debt gets so big that repayment looks impossible: the borrower sees no problem making it even bigger. Impossible is impossible, after all, so they might as well suffer under a gargantuan impossible sum instead of a merely huge one. Once you owe a million, what's another hundred thousand? Adding to enormous debt becomes psychologically easier the bigger that debt becomes. Just ask Congress.

The drive to consume spun out of control when houses became the ATMs of debt distribution. In 1974, household debt in the United States came to 60 percent of disposable income. What do you think it hit in 2008? An unbelievable 134 percent, which weighed in at $14.5 trillion. First Rule of Finance, anyone?

So, the subprime time bombs piled up at banks, which made the bankers uneasy, and they decided to get bad mortgages off the books. They locked a bunch of PhD propeller-capped heads in a room and refused to let them out until they came up with an inventive way to get rid of the subprime time bombs. The sophisticated gang in the room noticed that mortgage-backed securities, or MBSs, were popular among investors. They were created by securitizing mortgages, which means turning them into a security like a stock or a bond that can be easily traded in a market. Before securitization, it's hard to sell and resell a mortgage or any other type of loan because of the messy paperwork involved in transferring the payment agreement from lender A to lender B. Why bother with all that? Just make the loan into a stock or bond and start trading it.

From that starting point of MBSs, the geniuses invented collateralized debt obligations, or CDOs, to clean the books. They took a pool of subprime time bombs and combined them into one unit. Then they sliced the group into various levels by credit rating. One slice was called a tranche, which means slice in French. Using English would have made things too understandable to those outside the business. The top tranche had a beautiful credit rating of AAA, the tranches in the middle had lower ratings, and the bottom tranche was the riskiest pile of crap imaginable and would be sold off as an equity, like a stock. The bulk of nonpayment and default would happen in that bottom cesspool of an equity tranche, so the others could be sold off as lower-risk bonds. Here's how a $500 million CDO might have looked:

- $400 million AAA super-senior tranche
- $40 million A-rated senior tranche
- $40 million BB mezzanine tranche
- $20 million equity tranche

Whenever a few subprime time bombs exploded, they'd be contained in the bottom $20 million and the upper tranches would be fine. Even if the explosions spread beyond the equity tranche, they'd be contained by the BB mezzanine tranche, and if *that* couldn't contain them, then the A-rated senior tranche certainly could. Yep, that AAA super-senior tranche was as good as gold. In the beginning, when the debt dopes frolicked among their teaser payments, the default rate on subprime mortgages was less than 5 percent. No sweat!

Just to be sure as many tendrils of the financial system got wrapped up in this as possible, monoline insurers came on the scene. They make their money guaranteeing bonds and were tired of missing out on all that easy real-estate profit, so they moseyed onto CDO turf. Their backing allowed banks to turn a AA rating into a AAA, just like that. Yes, as the quality of lending went down, the ratings on tranches of CDOs went up. Makes you wonder why we even bother with ratings agencies and insurance companies, doesn't it?

From CDOs came credit default swaps, or CDSs. They transferred default risk from the schmuck holding the bag of junk assets to the protection seller. The schmuck paid a fee to the protection seller, and was then protected against the junk assets blowing up. If they did, the protection seller would cover any damages.

The next brilliant idea was structured investment vehicles, or SIVs. They were even more meaningless than their predecessors, as they issued short-term, high-quality paper backed by long-term, low-quality assets like CDOs. If you're wondering how anything backed by low-quality assets can be considered high quality, you're not qualified to work in a bank. You're just not smart enough.

I know it will come as a shock, but this well-built, solid, unshakable tower of financial triumph swayed one day in a breeze. That breeze came from a deadbeat calling it quits on his mortgage payments. Then his neighbor joined, then the next neighbor, then the whole street, the ward, the city, the state, and the nation, twisting that once-gentle breeze into an EF5 super tornado that took the tower down.

What led the first deadbeat to call it quits? Falling home prices. In response to demand for houses created by the free-wheeling debt distribution, home builders went nuts, too. They churned out homes at a pace that finally proved too much even for out-of-control consumers, and in 2006 a surplus of unsold homes weighed on the market. Prices peaked, then came down a tad as everybody held their breath, then crashed to Earth in a chorus of screams. Deadbeats who tried refinancing their homes at the end of their teaser rates found that the lower market value of their homes made it impossible. Their deadbeat natures finally came to the fore when they just stopped making payments, and started blaming everybody else involved in the whole mess. That unholy Federal Reserve. These sneaky bankers. Those dastardly financial wizards. How dare they force honest Americans into this penury!

Thoughts On Money

What this country needs is a good five-cent nickel. —Frank Adams

Can anybody remember when the times were not hard, and money not scarce? —Ralph Waldo Emerson

People are living longer than ever before, a phenomenon undoubtedly made necessary by the 30-year mortgage. —Doug Larson

The only reason a great many American families don't own an elephant is that they have never been offered an elephant for a dollar down and easy weekly payments. —Mad magazine

A man has one hundred dollars and you leave him with two dollars, that's subtraction. —Mae West

There is a very easy way to return from a casino with a small fortune: go there with a large one. —Jack Yelton

The vicious cycle spun tighter. Banks foreclosed on homes, which increased the supply overhang, which kept prices falling, which made it harder for more deadbeats to refinance their way out of their predicament, which led to them stopping payments, which brought more foreclosures, and on it went.

Meanwhile, back at the banks with their rooms full of PhD propeller-capped heads, all hell broke loose when those risk models built on a 5 percent default rate among subprime borrowers proved a tad naive. The deadbeats blew up not just the bottom CDO tranche, not just the mezzanine tranche, not just the senior tranche, but every single tranche. When deadbeats go down, they go down hard and they go down en masse because they're the most pathetic collection of monkey-see, monkey-do people you'll ever meet. The propeller-capped heads never thought of that. The stupidity of the masses is useful to a point, but does have its downside.

From all this, the media picked up on two things. First, the collection of toxic financial instruments created by banks—the CDOs, CDSs, MBSs, and SIVs you just read about—which they began referring to as an alphabet soup of toxic assets. Second, the sad plight of good folks who had been unfairly tricked by the Federal Reserve's easy money policy and banks' overzealous mortgage terms and housing prices that should never have fallen.

The media's much-hated alphabet soup was missing one key ingredient, though. In fact, it's the ingredient more central to the crisis than any other. Without the missing ingredient, none of what happened could have happened. Can you guess what ingredient the media missed?

FSPs.

FSPs are financially stupid people, and they started it all. Without financially stupid people signing onto loans that made no sense, the excess liquidity pumped out by the Fed and the absurd loans floated by banks would have gone nowhere. A bad loan without a borrower inflicts no damage. None! Like a cup of poison without a drinker, the damage is precisely zero. In America, though, a legion of lips willingly drank deep from that cup of toxic alphabet soup, and would later complain about the bellyache.

Yes, the government made mistakes. Yes, the banks are greedy, scheming knaves. Yes, the financial services industry is filled with chiselers. The only surprise, though, is that anybody is still surprised by these facts. It's always been this way. Government, banks, and speculators have caused financial problems since creation. Maybe we should blame schools for not teaching financial history better, or at all.

Let's take a quick jaunt down financial memory lane.

Financial Memory Lane

The Panic of 1907 occurred when copper-magnate-turned-banker Augustus Heinze and his brother, Otto, tried and failed to corner the market in United Copper Company stock. Otto bought a raft of shares to drive up the price and intended to then demand that short sellers cover their bets by buying shares from the only guy who owned them: him. He'd be able to name his price if he was the only holder. Too bad he wasn't. The short sellers found other sources of United Copper shares. The stock fell from $60 to $10 in two days. That killed Otto's brokerage firm and his brother's State Savings Bank of Butte, Montana. Augustus was also the president of the Mercantile National Bank in New York City, and his connection sparked a run on that bank that turned into a run on several New York banks and the near collapse of the New York Stock Exchange. John D. Rockefeller the oil man, J. P. Morgan the banker, several other bankers, and the U.S. Treasury ponied up $55 million to stabilize banks and trusts and keep depositors calm. Hmm, financial shenanigans bringing down banks and requiring bailout money from other banks and the Treasury? Where've we heard that recently?

Speculators sent the stock market to nosebleed levels in the 1920s, touting a new technology called radio and the growing automotive industry. Hundreds of thousands of

Americans were drawn to the stock market, and many borrowed money to buy even more stock than they could afford with cash alone. The borrowed money sent prices even higher, which attracted more people, who borrowed more money, which sent prices higher still. The "unstoppable" growth not only stopped, it crashed in 1929 and sent the U.S. and global economy to the mat, and was partly responsible for the Great Depression of the 1930s. Anything that rises too high too fast, whether tulips or stocks or home prices, is destined to fall back. Regression to the mean, it's called. Watch out for it. Another sure sign of disaster is when prices rise on borrowed money, which you may recall was a key part of America's rising real estate market in the early 2000s.

U.S. savings and loan institutions were deregulated in 1982, and immediately moved beyond their safe mortgage lending roots to paying higher interest rates for deposits, borrowing money from the Fed, making commercial loans, and even issuing credit cards. They also jumped into the booming real estate market of that time by taking partial ownership of many of the projects they financed. To grow their businesses as quickly as possible, they began relying on deposit brokers. The S&Ls all offered high rates to attract as much of the brokered deposit money as possible, then had to engage in riskier investments to keep up with their own high rates of payout. Brokers sensed opportunity, and pulled together a scam called "linked financing" in which one would promise to deliver a large deposit to an S&L *if* the S&L agreed to lend money to certain people or invest in certain products. The broker, of course, benefited by either sending its own people to borrow from the S&L or getting a commission on the product the S&L invested in. For example, junk bond king Michael Milken traded brokered deposits with S&Ls in exchange for their buying junk bonds from his clients. Let's see, unscrupulous brokers directing bank capital into bad assets. Anything familiar here? I wonder why S&Ls went bankrupt. The government had to step in to pay off deposits and sell assets through the Resolution

Trust Corporation it set up specifically to liquidate the S&Ls. Remember this example, because we'll later hear from a man who helped write rules to handle fraudulent banks during the S&L crisis, only to see them broken in the subprime mortgage meltdown.

Former head of bond trading at Salomon Brothers, John Meriwether, joined with Nobel Prize–winners Robert Merton and Myron Scholes in 1994 to set up a hedge fund called Long-Term Capital Management to profit off their belief that interest rates on various government bonds would converge in the long run, and that small short-term differences could be exploited. LTCM's theory of rate convergence worked beautifully—right up to the moment that it didn't. That's how all schemes go, by the way, and is worth bearing in mind. Russia defaulted on its government bonds in August 1998, investors jumped ship from various government bonds to the safety of U.S. Treasury bonds, and interest rate differences between bonds exploded. LTCM was caught in a trap and over-leveraged, and the Fed had to convince top U.S. banks to cobble together a $3.7 billion rescue package to keep the hedge fund from collapsing and dragging down the U.S. credit market, which would have sent interest rates sharply higher.

Detect a pattern yet? Financial markets are made up of fallible people plagued by human weaknesses like greed and dishonesty. They will *never* be clean. Do yourself a favor and stop trusting them.

Does the United States need to better regulate banks and financial markets? Yes, but the government says that after every blow-up. They enact new rules, a few good years go by, banks and other financial institutions say the rules are no longer needed because everything is going so well, the government clowns who don't know a thing about finance in the first place cave in to pressure from financial lobbyists to relax the rules, the abominable banks and financial fools and sap-headed speculators run wild and inflate yet another bubble, then everybody is surprised and outraged when the bubble bursts. It has always gone like this, and always will.

Waiting for government and banks to set the financial system right is like waiting for spiders to stop eating flies. Spiders eat flies, end of story. Government and banks screw up financial systems, end of story. It's what they do. You won't go wrong picturing the financial system as a house of cards, and will do well to remember that bankers' and politicians' knowledge of card houses leans more toward the making of them than the preventing of their collapse.

Get this through your head: no government rule will ever do more for you than the First Rule of Finance. If you break that, no rule from government will save you. Stop looking for government protection, stop expecting goodwill from bankers, stop leaving important parts of your life in the hands of others. Take control by following the First Rule and controlling the Three Cs *on your own*. You don't need anybody's help to do it.

Key contributors to almost every financial bubble are easy money, lots of debt, speculation that drives up prices, rising prices that attract more speculators, more speculators that need more money to borrow, and more borrowed money that drives up prices even more. Financial firms will always hire lobbyists to put politicians in their pockets. Politicians will always give in to incentives and bribes. Financial firms will always be let loose. Once let loose, they will always run wild and offer more debt than people should accept, and encourage rampant speculation. When it all falls down again, politicians will act "spitting mad" at the irresponsible financial industry—even as they use money from their tax-paying constituents to prop up their friends in finance. Together, government and financial firms take money from rubes in the creation of the problem, and again in its solution using tax proceeds, and the rubes are too stupid to ever figure it out.

Stop Getting Tricked

Rather than get tricked time and again, why not be smart? If you simply follow the First Rule of Finance, they can't get you. They can try to blow up the economy by getting people in hock up to their ears, but they won't succeed if everybody declines.

John Cassidy wrote in the March 16, 2009, issue of *The New Yorker* "The problem comes down to how to deal with the banks' 'toxic assets'—distressed mortgage bonds and mortgage-related derivatives, mostly—which have been festering on their balance sheets for nearly two years."[1] As far as the government rescue was concerned, Cassidy was right. But, why did those mortgage-related assets turn toxic in the first place? Because the mortgage payments weren't made. Why weren't they made? Because financial lame-brains couldn't figure out how much house they could afford. Let's not beat around the bush. The *real* toxic asset festers much farther down the mortgage food chain. Initially, it wasn't the financier who created the mortgage-backed securities; nor the next one who figured out how to slice, dice, and resell them around the world; nor the bank that offered bad terms to the borrower. Nope, ultimately, it was the dipstick holding the signing pen who couldn't figure out that the deal on paper wasn't right for him.

"Sorry," he could have said, "I can't afford these payments."

"But they're small for the first two years," the broker jerk would have replied.

"I see that," the smart borrower could have said, "but it's what happens after those first two years that worries me. I need a steady monthly payment, and I need it smaller than these. I have to pass."

Hallelujah! Repeated millions of times, that's all it would have taken to avoid the housing bubble and its aftermath, and the bad loan deals would have died out quickly. You know why? Because as soon as banks realized people weren't going to fall for terrible terms, they'd have stopped offering. They only offered these terms because idiots accepted them, again, and again, and again.

Gosh, how could the poor unwashed masses have ever avoided being duped by unscrupulous mortgage brokers and bad banks? How could they have seen through the sales pitches and the smoke and mirrors and arrived at any semblance of a good decision? "What should I do?" calls out the babe in swaddling clothes holding trembling pen to paper.

Um, read the contract?

I'd start there. Signing something used to mean that you'd read and agreed to it. These days, it apparently means only that the paper was slid across the desk to a poised pen. "Where do I sign?" is all anybody knows how to say anymore. Again, not too hard to grasp: first read, *then* sign. Say it with me, "First read, *then* sign."

How about a mnemonic device? When somebody says, "*Sign* here," think of your signature as a *sign* that you read the darned thing. Haven't read it yet? Then don't leave a sign that you have.

For subprime rubes, it probably would have been a good idea to calculate not just the ability to pay the first 24 payments, but all the rest after that. Whaddaya think? Had subprime rubes taken a moment—or two, or however many needed—to read the contracts in front of them, they would have noticed their payments being laughably low for two years, then suddenly increasing after that.

"Say, honey," a rube could have mumbled to a nearby spouse upon discovering the ramp-up in the interest rate. "These first 24 payments look like a slam dunk. It's payments from 25 and on that worry me. Lookee here."

The spouse leans over to behold the jump from payment 24 to payment 25.

"My, my, you're right. We can't afford those."

Even if the payment schedule wasn't that explicit, surely the word "adjustable" or "variable" in front of "interest rate" should have aroused curiosity. What if, just what if, the rate were to adjust or vary its way *upward*? Might have been worth thinking about.

The no-longer-a-rube could have then put down the dangerous pen, looked across the desk at the smiling poison vendor, and said, "Sorry, this won't work for us. We can handle the first two years, but not the years after that, so I can't sign. We're out."

Didn't happen. One rube after another signed on the line, and a catastrophe was born. They called themselves victims, but we know better. They were too stupid or lazy to read the contract into which they entered voluntarily, and then unable to honor their side of the bargain. Did they deserve the house of their dreams? Puh-lease. They barely deserved the pen they signed with.

A Pathetic Picture

In October 2007, Allan Sloan wrote in *Fortune* about a mortgage-backed security called GSAMP Trust 2006-S3. GSAMP stood for Goldman Sachs Alternative Mortgage Products. It contained 8,274 second-mortgage loans. Homeowners going for second mortgages are the dumbest of the dumb, experts at adding debt on top of debt, especially if they have little equity in the home from which to borrow for the second mortgage.

Knowing what you now know about financial dumbbells, how much equity do you think this pathetic parade had in their homes? "Probably just the 20 percent down payment," you might venture. Down payment? Come on, now, you know these dopes don't bother with down payments. "Then, maybe half that," you think. Ten percent? For this clod collection? "Fine, then I'll go with half of *that*." You have a kind heart, I'll say that about you, but you still don't understand the depth of idiocy we're dealing with.

The average equity these flounders had in their homes was 0.71 percent. I know, you think I made a mistake on the keyboard and it's supposed to read 7.1 percent, but I didn't. They had just 0.71 percent equity. Loans accounted for 99.29 percent of their home values.

Yet they went for *another* loan.

How could such an odd mob get any loan? By lying. The industry even adopted an unofficial term for such a mortgage; they called it a "liar's loan." Around 58 percent of the loans were low-documentation or no-documentation, so the majority of the gang could have written anything they wanted about their supposed income—or nothing at all—and still received their mortgage. So that's what they did.

The excuse factory kicked into high gear in 2006 when housing prices fell and the squatters found themselves in a pickle. "I can't make my payments, I can't refinance, I can't sell at a profit, I can't do anything from this position," they cried. Right, but who walked into the position? Shouldn't an adult understand that owing 99 percent of the value of something that fluctuates in price is risky? Sure they should. Owning less than 1 percent looks a little, oh I don't know, reckless? Poised for perfection, I'd say, and only children can be excused for expecting perfection. Adults build in margin for error, and less than 1 percent ain't much margin.

We can just picture the scene that started it all, the one that put the rubes in the position from which they'd later complain. Mainstream media sympathized with the impossible position, but didn't bother to examine its creation, so let's cover it here. This scene is called Rodney Rube's Big Day, and it takes place in the office of No-Doc Disasters where Rodney has just taken off his FSP baseball cap and sat down with mortgage broker Sly Sal.

"You know," Rodney says after they shake hands, "I really want to buy a house but I don't have any money for a down payment, or monthly payments for that matter. Think you can help me?"

"Of course," Sal says. "Listen, the beauty of home prices these days is that they always go up, so we're not doing down payments anymore. Surprise!"

"No kidding? I always heard from my folks that I needed 20 per—"

"Right, the old 20 percent thing. Well, times change, what can I say? Gone!" He laughs and looks at Rodney until they both laugh together. "Oh, golly. So, you won't need that, and we'll get you started with a super low interest rate for a couple of years to ease you into the mortgage. Your payments will probably be lower than what you're paying now for rent."

"Cool."

"We'll raise the payments in a couple of years. Will that work?"

"Yeah, whatever. Oh, one thing, though," Rodney says in a lower voice.

"What's that?"

"My employer is a fly-by-night outfit and won't be able to confirm my job history. Is that okay?"

Sal waves his hand with another smile.

"No sweat. We've all been there, right? Am I right? We'll hook you up with our special Liar's Loan with almost no documentation. To hell with your employer. You can verify your own job and income."

"This place is sweet!" Rodney says. "It's so easy."

"You bet it is." Sal leans in a little closer. "See, we don't do the actual lending." He winks. "A bank handles that, so we couldn't care less whether you repay the loan!"

"What a riot!"

"I know! We just set up terms that work for you, then toss the file to a bank and get our commission. No matter what happens after that, we've got our money."

"Awesome!" Rodney shouts.

"You said it!"

"Where do I sign?"

Sal slides only the last page of the contract across the desk and points with his pen to a line over the word *Buyer*. "Right here, and you'll be a new homeowner."

"Okay."

Do you still feel sorry for Rodney when he can't make payments, can't refinance, can't sell at a profit, and complains that he "can't do anything from this position"? Poor Rodney in the media is Pathetic Rodney in real life.

Some bankers are creeps, without a doubt. They'll do anything to tick up another percent of profit. But, 'twas always thus, folks. It's a wooly world out there, and nobody cares as much about your money as you do. Buyer beware, borrower beware, and overall just be aware.

Banksters in Action

Aaron Sweyne worked for 15 years in the subprime credit-card division of a major bank in the upper midwestern United States, and sent me in 2009 the story of his experience. He couldn't share the bank's name, but told me it was "one of the big ones and, yes, they took TARP money and were in the news every day during the crisis." TARP stands for Troubled Asset Relief Program, the government's $700 billion bailout of bad banks. You'll read more about it later.

Aaron sold a credit-card-accessible home equity line of credit with no closing costs and a quick process so people could enjoy "easy access to their home equity." He was amazed by the variety of ways people "justified tapping their home equity. Most of the time, customers already had $20k to $30k of unsecured credit card debt, so consolidating on a home equity loan reduced their monthly payments, put all payments into one, and often gave them a lower rate and tax deductibility. Not a bad value proposition on the surface, kind of a 'lesser of two evils' decision, but very few people had the discipline to consolidate the debt, then *not* run up the old credit cards again."

They charged their cards to the moon, moved the balance over to what they owed on their home, then charged the cards to the moon again. I wonder why that couldn't go on forever? The worst part is that the dopes doing it really *did* wonder why it couldn't go on forever, and whined when it ended. That's no coincidence, naturally. It was just such ignoramuses that Aaron's bank and many others wanted to snag. They couldn't get smart people to sign up for the asininity, so they went after financially stupid people, and found them by the boatload.

Aaron remembered that his bank's number-one lead source for many years was the list of "people who already had an equity line but wanted an increased limit so they could pay off more debt again!" The second-best source was the list of chowderheads who signed up for an unsecured credit card in response to a phone call from the sales center. They got enticed once, after all, why not again?

The bank's tactics finally got to Aaron, making him regret his career choice. "In the beginning," he recalled, "I thought it was a noble career, working for a prestigious financial institution. 'Helping people succeed financially' was what we were supposed to be doing." Had the bank shot straight, its slogan would have read, "Helping people hang themselves financially." Toward the end of his career in 2007, Aaron wanted to tell every customer, "Stop borrowing money, spend less than you make, get an emergency fund saved up, get out of debt, and *then* you will succeed financially."

What was most disturbing to him? "We only made money if customers were continually adding debt, moving debt around, or replacing a competitor's debt with our debt. There was always a debate over 'how much debt is too much for our customers?' We gathered lots of research, data that would suggest this much unsecured debt with incomes of this much were the line in the sand. But never was it suggested that maybe we shouldn't be actively marketing to people to get them to *add* to their debt. Maybe we should just have these products available for customers who *asked* for them? Maybe we shouldn't be telemarketing, internet marketing, direct mailing, emailing, and hundreds of other techniques with the single goal of getting customers to take on more debt?"

Maybe. Then again, nah. Desperately seeking stupids is just way too profitable. Drawing on his experience, Aaron thinks succeeding in the credit card business is "really quite simple." He breaks it down into three steps.

First, "issue more cards [this year] than you did the year before. You have to grow receivables."

Second, "lend money to people who just barely qualify for the loan. If you go completely conservative with your lending on credit cards, the upper end of customers are too smart to carry a balance or pay high rates or fees—they will not use your card and you will make no money. Lend money to the lowest end of the spectrum, and your loss rates will be too high to make money. Find the people in the *lower-middle*, and you can make money."

Third, create "a sales culture focused on getting customers to use their cards. Contests and commissions motivate the sales force, marketing creates the message for customers: 'You deserve a break, take that vacation, buy some new clothes, it's back-to-school time, it's summertime, today is the best time to *buy something*!'"

When the kettle of fish finally boiled over and government stepped in to bail out the bad banks, Aaron's company shut down his entire sales division. He took his severance package and moved on, happy for "a way out of this crazy business." As for the bank, do you suppose it learned the error of its ways and will now put as much effort into encouraging saving as it once put into encouraging debt?

Get real. According to Aaron, "The company realized it could not conservatively lend its way out of the hole it was in and grow the business—the math just didn't work. It was better to hunker down, let the portfolio run off, and wait for better times to start all over again." Yes, the bank will be back in action one of these years, using the same poppycock to rope the same pinheads into the same predicament. Wait and see.

The culture of debt is so pervasive, it even snagged Aaron and his family. You'll read later how they managed to escape and live free. Too many people, however, never do.

CHAPTER 4

The Society You're Up Against

Just because somebody offers you something doesn't mean you have to take it. Just because a company makes a new gadget doesn't mean you have to buy it. Just because everybody else carries a balance on 13 credit cards doesn't mean you have to have more than one credit card or carry a balance. Just because the government wants you to spend money on trifles you don't need—to generate sales tax and keep people employed at manufacturing trifles—doesn't mean you have to do it.

The American economy is a fraud.

It's based on unnecessary consumption financed by debt. Government and big business love that because it keeps all the suckers at jobs they hate to service the debt they amassed to buy things they don't need. People without debt are free to find work they enjoy, and that freedom leads to time away from jobs and lower income tax revenue. Can't have that! People who live within their means spend less, which keeps company profits down and lowers corporate tax revenue and sales tax revenue. Can't have that! Government and big business don't like people who manage their finances well, which is why you see millions of creative ways to blow your money everywhere you turn.

In this chapter, and the next two, we look at the many ways that government, banks, and big business work together to create a money-trap society. We'll explore areas beyond finance to see the pattern at work, and understand how society's very design is intended to extract as much money from citizens as possible. Social issues, exciting rallies, and alluring advertisements are all just showmanship to conceal the constant wealth transfer from individuals to government, banks, and big business.

Keeping You in Debt

Debt is control. If they can keep you in debt, they can control you. "They" are the financial people everywhere in government, banking, and big business who maintain a thousand on-ramps to the interstate of indentureship. How many people have you heard say they hate their jobs? Probably a lot. The next time you hear it, ask, "Then why don't you get a different one?" You're guaranteed to hear something along the lines of "Because I need the money."

Why?

It's not a silly question. We all have bills. We all have cars. We all have homes. We all need income to pay for those. However, once an initial base of cash is established and grown via the First Rule of Finance and controlling the Three Cs, financial freedom arrives on a white horse. It's possible to obtain it in less than 10 years, as you'll read later. The decade of our 20s, for example, is a fine time to use our first real job to pay off school debt, adopt smart financial habits, and build a cash base.

Financially free people don't *need* money right now because they've already set some aside. People with solid finances don't spend even a week at a job they don't like. They find a new one. If they don't like that one, they find a different one. Eventually, they either find a job they like or they create it. They make their income from the life they want, instead of cobbling together a mean little tale of survival at a job they hate.

People in debt don't have that luxury. They have to service the debt. They *need* money right now. They can't go any period of time without income because they have no reserves, so they're stuck at a crummy job with—and this is no coincidence—automatic tax deductions. Almost all jobs include automatic tax deductions. Self-employment does not. It takes a base of capital to embark on self-employment. What's the best way to limit people's ability to become self-employed? Keep them in debt. Starting to get the picture?

This is not a conspiracy, but just the natural balance that comes from different groups figuring out how to tease money from financially stupid people, then taking the successful methods to extremes. The parts of society that feed off the stupidity of the masses steadily perfected the art of sucking money out of them, and locked the best methods in place.

Government realized that taxation happens best when it happens automatically, so people don't even notice how much they pay out of each check. That's why almost every ability to reduce income tax payments is available only to the self-employed. Business owners enjoy great flexibility in allocating their income toward profitable activity *before* incurring taxes. Payroll chumps just pay. That doesn't mean all jobs are bad or that everybody needs to quit their jobs and start their own businesses. You may like a job you had before or one you have now. Just know that there's a reason government is so obsessed with the employment rate and wants you at a job every day, like it or not. They don't want jobs to look like choices, they want them to look like inevitable facts of life. People have been taught that jobs are necessities. They're not. They're just one way among many to earn an income, and smart people make a deliberate decision to earn their money the way they want to earn it, and then do so. That might be a good job, it might be something else. The point is that *they* choose how they want to live. Dummies just go anywhere, usually to a place they don't like, and complain that everybody has to do it. That's music to government ears.

Credit cards were a master stroke on the part of bankers. They really are pure genius. Almost nobody can grasp that swiped plastic and the numbers involved are real money, so consumers keep piling on debt, racking up the numbers and keeping them there, being charged interest forever. Voluntarily! The debt dopes keep paying their minimums while the interest keeps adding up, and I imagine bankers still chuckle and shake their heads at the steady stream of cash from clods. "Just keep it comin', guys," they say, and the dumb guys do.

Once big business saw the army of idiots with their new plastic cards, they had a field day dreaming up new ways for debt to accumulate. Credit cards took root in the 1950s, and that's also when fully enclosed shopping malls began replacing neighborhood stores, so cards could be used in one shop after another, without even a breath of outdoor air in between. Interesting timing, don't you think? Cities became sprawling collections of card-swiping stations, each in a different color with different goods arranged in different ways, but all running up the same numbers on the same cards.

So far, so good. The masses of morons were armed with cards and taught to trap themselves inside fully enclosed mall containers with nothing to do but swipe cards wherever they turned. Like bugs in a bottle, they bounced along the sidewalls of malls and swiped away. That's when prices detached from reality.

Once the debt dopes had been moved beyond cash, they no longer needed to consider their ability to afford things. They could afford anything because every price was just another number on the pile. Cars became expensive and always financed, and every member of the family got one. Even high school students began driving brand new cars. TVs got bigger. Every kid needed the latest electronic gizmo. Houses exploded in size.

Incomes stayed roughly the same, but spending and debt went through the roof. The luxury once tasted became a necessity, and everybody felt entitled to a life of shiny trifles. An ample supply of credit cards guaranteed they could get it, too.

And there you have it. An entire society enslaved. They think they have to work at jobs they don't like, pay taxes automatically, and use debt for every purchase. The trap is sprung. The debt prevents cash from accumulating. The lack of cash reserves makes the job necessary. The job automatically deducts taxes. The expectation to live a life full of shiny trifles keeps them running the debt ever higher, and the modern economy is in full swing.

Sure, *I'm* the crazy one, to point it out. The walking army of idiots with their cards isn't crazy. No, no. It's the ones who dare look on from the sidelines who must be crazy. The sane thing to do is show up at a job you hate to get a little bit of money after automatically paying taxes so you can make the minimum payment on 13 credit cards to keep them active and ready to buy more trifles you don't need and haul them in a car you can't afford to a home whose mortgage payments eat up half your income. That's the sane thing, all right.

Solving Runaway Debt by Borrowing

The government seems to think so. You know what the top order of the day was when the economy crumbled under a mountain of defaulted mortgage debt? To stimulate borrowing and spending. Yes, the runaway debt problem was to be solved by borrowing unprecedented amounts of money from other countries to encourage banks to start lending again and consumers to start borrowing and spending again. Following this line of thinking, you can get over alcoholism with a stiff shot of whiskey, put out a fire with a bucket of gasoline, clean a floor by scattering dirt on it, and stop domestic violence by beating your children.

Leading the way, the government itself put together in early 2009 a plan to borrow more than $9 trillion on top of the $11 trillion it already owed. The nonpartisan Congressional Budget Office concluded that the national debt would grow by about $1 trillion per year to exceed 82 percent of the entire economy by 2019, and threaten the nation's financial stability. That led Senate Budget Committee senior Republican Judd Gregg to say, "This clearly creates a scenario where the country's going to go bankrupt. It's almost that simple. One would hope these numbers would wake somebody up."

They won't. If debt levels could awaken the country, they would have done so decades ago. If debt addiction ranges from the federal government all the way down to Rodney Rube thinking he can get a new house with no down payment or proof of income, it's a systemic cancer. Even the numbers have become meaningless to the army of idiots. Let's make the debt trajectory easy to remember by calling it $20 trillion by 2020. A $20 trillion debt by 2020? So what? The number is so big it doesn't even fit on calculators without scientific notation. Tell people the country is headed toward 2×10^{13} dollars of debt, and only the folks at Caltech and MIT are nodding with you. Yes, the national debt is on its way to being so big we have to describe it the same way we describe distances to stars.

I considered it a four-alarm fire when U.S. debt hit $3 trillion. I was in college at that time, and wrote a paper about it saying that $1 trillion of debt had been la-la land, but now we were at *three times* that. Then it hit $5 trillion and I thought the riots would start at any moment. Then it hit $10 trillion and it was all I could do to steady myself. That was just a couple of years ago, but we're already talking about $20 trillion! The slack-jawed card-swipers stumbling from store to store are just as clueless on the way to their nation being $20 trillion in hock as they were on the way to it being $10 trillion in hock.

That takes us back to an earlier discussion. Remember all the crying by debt dopes that banks are unfair and government doesn't do enough to prevent people from spending themselves into oblivion? Look how goofy that notion appears now. We already established that the financial industry has always been and will always be out to get you. On top of that, we can add that government is too stupid to rein in its own runaway debt habit, so how can we expect it to help other addicts? We can't.

Washington's debt addiction may be its only true claim on bipartisanship. Both parties love debt, and so do popular and unpopular presidents alike. Politicians differ on how to spend money, but they agree on the need to spend mind-shattering sums of it.

Want to know how much of a financial friend you have in government? Consider Social Security and Medicare. Most people pay taxes into the programs and assume—quite reasonably, I should add—that government keeps it safe for them to use later in life when they're no longer working and their health has deteriorated. Wrong. Government has already blown the money on other projects. A pool of capital had no chance of surviving Washington's spendthrifts.

Don't take my word for it, take Paul O'Neill's. He served as Treasury secretary in 2001 and 2002. While serving, he commissioned a report showing the United States would face future federal budget deficits so huge that closing the budget gap would require an income-tax boost of 66 percent. When President Bush not only ignored runaway spending for the Iraq war and other initiatives, but also insisted on passing tax *cuts* for the wealthy, O'Neill resigned. William G. Gale and Peter Orszag at the Brookings Institution wrote in *The American Prospect* in April 2004 that the Bush tax cuts "shift the burden of taxation away from upper-income, capital-owning households and toward the wage-earning households of the lower and middle classes. For all but the wealthy, this will ultimately cause substantial harm. Shifting costs to future generations of workers to finance tax boons for today's owners of capital is unproductive, unfair, and unwise."

No wonder O'Neill called it quits. Here's what he told *Frontline* on November 24, 2008, when asked if Social Security and Medicare were intended to save for our retirement years:

> No. Since 1935 we've talked that talk, like we were saving money. We've been spending money all along. It's a giant fraud; it's a giant Ponzi scheme. Every year we took the money and we spent it on other things. There's a so-called famous lockbox in West Virginia I went to look at when I was Secretary of the Treasury. You know what's in the lockbox? Actually it's a filing cabinet, and there are some pieces of paper that say, 'We owe you.' There's no money there; there are no investments there. There's nothing there but a piece of paper. That's a fraud. People think, 'Hey, I put money all my life in Social Security and Medicare.' You didn't really. The government just took it and spent it on something else. There's no money there.[1]

That's the same government that people expect to protect them from borrowing and spending? Government can't get its own finances straight. It certainly won't help citizens manage theirs.

You Spend, They Profit

Moreover, government *wants* citizens to spend themselves into oblivion. There's a conflict of interest between what's good for you as an individual and what's good for the debt-based economy that Washington and big business have put in place over the years.

Look at what Federal Reserve Bank of San Francisco President Janet Yellen said in a March 2009 speech to the Forecasters Club of New York: ". . . consumers are pulling back on purchases, especially on durable goods, to build their savings. . . . Such precautions may be smart for individuals and firms, but they intensify economic distress for the economy as a whole."

What's that? You thought the economy as a whole included your interests? Don't be silly. Your duty is to spend at a breakneck pace, with your neck being the one breaking. You spend, they profit, that's how it goes in this economy as a whole. Maybe we should write "economy as a *hole*," down which you're supposed to throw every scrap of your wealth.

Keeping It Stupid

The following is adapted from an article I wrote at JasonKelly .com on September 20, 2008, called "Overheard at the Wall Street Bar & Grill." That month, insurance giant AIG was rescued by the Federal Reserve and U.S. Treasury, lenders Fannie Mae and Freddie Mac were saved by the Federal Housing Finance Agency, Lehman Brothers declared bankruptcy, and claims that some financial companies were too big to fail reached fever pitch. The $700-billion TARP bank bailout was announced three weeks later.

Barry Big sat with a vodka gimlet next to Sam Small, who was drinking a Bud Light. A TV over the bar reported the financial news and the two men watched it for a while without speaking.

"What a crock," Sam said at last. "Too big to fail? Then what are the rest of us, too small to matter?"

"Basically," Barry said. "If AIG and Fannie and Freddie had just collapsed, the financial system would have been catastrophically damaged."

"Whose financial system? Here's mine: go to work, get paid, pay my bills, leave what's left in the bank. How does a bunch of greedy folks out of work on Wall Street change any of my routines?"

"Are you serious?" Barry asked. He set down his glass and ran his fingers through his hair. "I hardly know where to begin.

(continued)

(continued)

Your financial system. Leave the money in the bank, eh? Guess what? A money market fund broke the buck, Sam. That means that your money isn't safe in banks anymore."

"Mine is, Barry. Checked it. Still there."

"What if it hadn't of been?"

"I'm insured. I think it's called the FDIC, left over from when another bunch of financial geniuses in suits kinda like yours ran the system into the ground. Anyway, there was no run on my bank."

"Yeah, well you're going to be hurt because it's your tax dollars keeping these guys who are too big to fail in business."

"So the only reason I get damaged is that my tax money is used to save their financial system so they can come back in a few years and destroy it again—on my dime. I have an idea: Don't bail 'em out."

Barry laughed. "You're a hayseed, Sam. I don't know how you can't see the freezing up of credit, mortgage availability, loan availability, and such as affecting everybody in the country."

"Like I said, I pay my bills. Nobody's foreclosing on me. I kept my credit cards at a zero balance, saved enough for years to make a 20 percent down payment on my house, made sure I could afford the monthly payment, and generally try to sock away 20 percent a month. I have all the credit I need, I have my mortgage already, I don't want any loans. All in all, I don't see the collapsing system doing much to my life."

Barry rolled his eyes. "The ignorance astounds me. It's people like you, Sam, who get us into messes like this. If only you knew something about finance."

"Yeah, if only, Barry. Running the country the way I run my life would just never work, would it? I may not know much about money, but it looks to me that your gang got just one part of the 'keep it simple, stupid' philosophy right."

"There was nothing simple about it."

Sam finished his beer and clapped Barry on the shoulder. "I know."

One can't help but wonder, though: If all that borrowing and spending were so good for the economy, then why did the whole thing nearly collapse from overwhelming debt? Maybe—and I know I'm out on a limb here—but just maybe, less borrowing and more saving would create financial strength.

You'd think that what's smart for individuals would be good for the economy, but no, according to our financial leaders, what's smart for individuals creates distress for the economy. Who do you suppose such an economy was designed to benefit? Not you, that's for sure. If you listen to messages from government, financial firms, and corporations you'll find yourself caught in their trap of borrowing and spending. Most people do listen, and most people are caught.

The Federal Reserve, AKA The Department of Inflation

The teeth of the borrowing and spending trap are bolted on by the Federal Reserve, which is not federal and has no reserves. That right there should tell you it's a slippery beast, hard to pin down as it slithers its way into every part of the economy by manipulating the monetary system. Guess who created it? Big bankers. To serve whom, do you suppose? Big bankers. With whom do they always work? Government.

In our jaunt down Financial Memory Lane earlier, you read about The Panic of 1907 that turned into a run on New York banks and forced bankers and the U.S. Treasury to bail out the system. That made bankers long for a central guarantor of all deposits to step in and prop up their rickety framework when it extended too far and collapsed. Bankers worked with Congress in 1908 to set up an exploratory group called the National Monetary Commission, and were kind enough to offer their own staffers to work it. Leading the team was Rhode Island Republican Senator

Nelson Aldrich, a man known for his wealthy banking and big-business connections, including his daughter's marriage to John D. Rockefeller, Jr. Thus, a group of foxes from the big banks of 100 years ago gathered to devise a way to take care of the chicken population.

The bulk of the planning happened in November 1910 at the Jekyll Island Club off the coast of Georgia, a resort partly owned by J. P. Morgan. It was very hush-hush, with Aldrich forcing all participants to pledge secrecy. They decided that, unlike European central banks, the U.S. model would be divided into 12 privately owned member banks to make the centralization harder for people to recognize. The group of 12 private banks would be overseen by a presidentially appointed board of governors, making a tidy public-private partnership. That partnership, now known as the Fed, would be given power to inflate the money supply to provide themselves and the economy with whatever cash was needed. That would enable banks to lend liberally with little concern for the consequences, because the new central bank would put out any bad debt fires with its cash hose.

The Fed deliberately uses language that's difficult for nonfinancial people to understand. Even its founding documents boggle most readers. The Federal Reserve Act of 1913 stated in its preamble that its purpose was "to provide for the establishment of Federal Reserve Banks, to furnish an elastic currency, to afford a means of rediscounting commercial paper" and other purposes. Welcome to Fedspeak. An elastic currency is money and credit that can be stretched or expanded, like elastic, any time the Fed wants. It can also be shrunk. Rediscounting is lending funds before outstanding loans have come due, as yet another way of using money before it exists. The Act granted a mostly private central bank the power to create money, control the money supply and interest rates, and lend money to the government at interest. A 1984 pamphlet from the Federal Reserve Bank of Boston called "Putting It Simply" stated,

"When you or I write a check there must be sufficient funds in our account to cover the check, but when the Federal Reserve writes a check there is no bank deposit on which that check is drawn. When the Federal Reserve writes a check, it is creating money." Most of the checks it writes are to buy U.S. Treasuries. The Fed creates money to lend to the Treasury, which is a debt that must be repaid with interest by taxpayers.

Can you imagine handing over such power to bankers, those most proven to abuse it? Many alive at the time of the Fed's creation could not, and many alive today cannot.

Minnesota Republican Congressman Charles Lindbergh served 10 years in the House from 1907 to 1917, and was a vocal opponent of the Act. He said, "When the president signs [the Federal Reserve Act of 1913], the invisible government by the money power—proven to exist by the Money Trust Investigation—will be legalized. The new law will create inflation whenever the trusts want inflation. From now on, depressions will be scientifically created." He called it the "worst legislative crime of the ages."[2]

The Federal Reserve Archival System for Economic Research (FRASER) provides this summary of the investigation referred to by Lindbergh:

> In 1912, a special subcommittee was convened by the Chairman of the House Banking and Currency Committee, Arsene P. Pujo. Its purpose was to investigate the "money trust," a small group of Wall Street bankers that exerted powerful control over the nation's finances. The committee's majority report concluded that a group of financial leaders had abused the public trust to consolidate control over many industries.

You can see why Lindbergh was so upset to find that the trust was not only allowed to continue operating, but sanctified by law only one year after being publicly exposed.

In his 2009 book *End the Fed,* Texas Republican Congressman Ron Paul wrote that the creation of the Fed was:

> a form of financial socialism that benefited the rich and the powerful. As for the excuse, it was then what it is now. The claim is that the Fed would protect the monetary and financial system against inflation and violent swings in market activity. It would stabilize the system by providing stimulus when it was necessary and pulling back on inflation when the economy became overheated.[3]

How'd that go? Not very well. Inflation from the Fed has steadily eroded the worth of a dollar, thereby stealing the value of citizen savings. It's another force pushing people to do something with their money other than save it. The public-private partnership that is the Fed has enabled government and banks to keep prices rising so people must work harder to keep up, and has made borrowing look like the best way to get ahead. Remember, the Fed can put as much cheap money on the street as it wants. When it does so, banks make lending easier and easier. Facing ever higher prices and ever easier loans over the past century, of course the population gravitated toward a life of borrowing.

Ron Paul wrote that, to see what the Fed has done:

> One only needs to reflect on the dramatic decline in the value of the dollar that has taken place since the Fed was established in 1913. The goods and services you could buy for $1.00 in 1913 now cost nearly $21.00. Another way to look at this is from the perspective of the purchasing power of the dollar itself. It has fallen to less than $0.05 of its 1913 value. We might say that the government and its banking cartel have together stolen $0.95 of every dollar as they have pursued a relentlessly inflationary policy.[4]

No wonder it's hard to get ahead in America.

Let's turn to another expert to see just how hard. Elizabeth Warren is a professor at Harvard Law School and the chair of the Congressional Oversight Panel for the Troubled Asset Relief Program, the plan that spent $700 billion of taxpayer money to bail out banks. She told *The Washington Post*[5] in October 2009 that inflation has kept middle-class income shrinking for a generation. For example, "a fully employed male today earns on average about $800 less, adjusted for inflation, than a fully employed male earned a generation ago." How did families survive? They "put a second earner into the workforce and, of course, that's now flattened out because there aren't any more people to put into the workforce."

Meanwhile, thanks to that same inflation sponsored by the Fed, households need to spend more on their core expenses of housing, health insurance, child care, transportation, and taxes. Warren said that "families are spending a lot more on what you describe as 'the basic nut.'"

In this triangle of tribulation, we find incomes down, expenses up, and . . . what do you suppose describes the third component? Debt. That was the solution most families chose. Warren said that to "deal with" falling incomes and rising expenses, families "stopped saving and started going into debt."

She concluded that the debt "really means that we have a middle class that a generation ago we would have described as solid, secure, dependable. If you could just get into the middle class, you could pretty much count on a fairly comfortable life and all the way through to a comfortable retirement. That's been hollowed out. Sure, there are people who are going to make it through just fine, but the vulnerability of families in the middle class has just—it has gone up enormously."

Do you think the Fed gives a hoot about that? No. It helped engineer it. Before the December 2009 confirmation of Ben Bernanke for a second term as Federal Reserve chairman, Rhode Island Democratic Senator Sheldon Whitehouse said he wanted to hear that the Fed would avert its eyes from "an exclusive gaze on the welfare of Wall Street and start giving a red-hot damn about the American public." Unfortunately, the Fed *is* Wall Street. It'll stop caring for Wall Street's welfare the same day water runs uphill.

The part played by the Fed banking cartel doesn't excuse people who used debt to fund extravagance, but it does show the origin of the pressure and temptation to do so. If people had resisted the debt-based lifestyle from the start, it never would have taken root. They didn't resist. Instead of scaling back spending as prices rose, they scaled up borrowing to keep living the same way, or more lavishly. Rather than refusing higher costs, they financed them. They charged the American dream on credit cards. The once makeshift measure of borrowing became woven into the flag to which we pledge allegiance, and all the bankers laughed.

The money trust's power grab, kicked off almost a hundred years ago with the founding of the Fed, has gone pretty well. Money floated to the top of society, leaving desperation and debt below.

5

Government of the Corporations, by the Corporations, for the Corporations

If Abraham Lincoln were to give today an amended presentation of his Gettysburg Address delivered on November 19, 1863, he'd need to reword his famous conclusion to something along these lines: "The cause for which so many died nobly to advance—government of the people, by the people, for the people—has perished from the earth. In its stead we find a carcass of the nation our fathers brought forth on this continent, a government of the corporations, by the corporations, for the corporations."

Prepare for a closer look at that carcass.

Government and Banks in Bed

The subprime mortgage crisis proved just how cozily government and banks lie in bed together to spawn the economy of their liking. During the savings and loan scandal of the late 1980s (S&L crisis), which you read about in our walk down Financial Memory Lane in Chapter 3, a regulator named William K. Black exposed government connections to bank fraud when he accused then–house speaker Jim Wright and five U.S. senators, including John Glenn and John McCain, of doing favors for the S&Ls in exchange for political contributions. Black wrote a book about the experience, aptly titled *The Best Way to Rob a Bank Is to Own One*. On April 3, 2009, he appeared on *Bill Moyers Journal*[1] to discuss the subprime mortgage crisis.

Black said the meltdown was driven by fraud, which he defined as deceiving the public by creating trust and then betraying it. He said the fraud began in CEO offices, and Moyers asked him how the CEOs did it. Black said they made bad loans because they pay better, they grew rapidly in a Ponzi-like scheme, and they employed massive leverage. He explained:

> That just means borrowing a lot of money, and the combination creates a situation where you have guaranteed record profits in the early years. That makes you rich, through the bonuses that modern executive compensation has produced. It also makes it inevitable that there's going to be a disaster down the road.

He said some bank CEOs deliberately made bad loans to boost their own personal income. To do so, they subordinated internal controls such as accounting checks and balances to cook the books for their purposes. By now, you know that banking and finance have always been plagued by such swindlers. What you need to understand, though, is that government helps the swindlers, not you. The honest citizen expects government to punish criminal CEO behavior. It doesn't. In fact, it encourages criminal CEO behavior when it produces big profits that can be partially directed into political coffers. Politicians don't care where their funding comes from. Cynicism spelled differently is A-W-A-R-E-N-E-S-S.

As proof, consider that just when lenders spun most wildly out of control, government in Washington stopped regulating. Black told Moyers that the Bush administration essentially got rid of regulation, enabling banks to make bad loans with impunity because no regulators looked.

Law enforcement caught on, though. The FBI publicly warned in September 2004 that there was an epidemic of mortgage fraud that would produce a crisis at least as bad as the S&L crisis if it was allowed to continue. However, following the 9/11 attacks, the Justice Department transferred 500 white-collar crime specialists in the FBI to national terrorism. The result, Black said, was that the FBI faced a financial crisis possibly 1,000 times worse, certainly 100 times worse, than the S&L crisis, but with only one-fifth as many agents as worked the S&L crisis. No wonder they couldn't stop it.

That left law enforcement unable to help. What about lawmakers? They spent more time with bank lobbyists than bank regulators. Moyers talked about a 2003 photograph of five men in suits standing around a stack of documents tied in red tape. Behind them was wallpaper with the words "Cutting Red Tape" in several places. The men held a chainsaw and some pruning shears against the red tape. Who were the men? James Gilleran from the Office of Thrift Supervision, FDIC Chairman John Reich, and three bank trade representatives: Harry Doherty of America's Community Bankers, Ken Guenther of the Independent Community Bankers of America, and James McLaughlin of the American Bankers Association. About the photo, Black said:

> They're the lobbyists for the bankers. And everybody's grinning. The government's working together with the industry to destroy regulation. Well, we now know what happens when you destroy regulation. You get the biggest financial calamity of anybody under the age of 80.

Black pointed out that Bill Clinton's Treasury secretaries, Robert Rubin and Lawrence Summers, blocked attempts to regulate the exotic derivatives that would later be known as toxic assets. He said they "came together to say not only will we block this particular regulation, we will pass a law that says you can't regulate. And it's this type of derivative that is most involved in the AIG scandal. AIG all by itself cost the same as the entire savings and loan debacle."

AIG stands for American International Group. It's one of the largest insurance companies in the world, with operations in over 130 countries. In September 2008, its derivative portfolio collapsed in the subprime mortgage meltdown, its credit rating dropped, and it received in 2008 and 2009 some $182 billion in government assistance because it was deemed systemically important. Important to whose system, though? After the dust cleared, we found out. In November 2009, Neil M. Barofsky, special inspector general for the Troubled Asset Relief Program, published his office's report on the AIG bailout. It found that the Federal Reserve Bank of New York "adopted in substantial part the economic terms of a draft term sheet under consideration by a consortium of private banks," and whom do you reckon those terms were designed to benefit?

About the report, Gretchen Morgenson wrote in the *New York Times*:

> The Fed, under [then–President of the Federal Reserve Bank of New York, but now U.S. Treasury Secretary Timothy] Geithner's direction, caved in to AIG's counterparties, giving them 100 cents on the dollar for positions that would have been worth far less if AIG had defaulted. Goldman Sachs, Merrill Lynch, Société Générale and other banks were in the group that got full value for their contracts when many others were accepting fire-sale prices. . . . The report said that while bailing out Goldman and other investment banks might not have been the intent behind the Fed's AIG rescue, it certainly was its effect.[2]

It was *banks* that decided whether and how the government should hand money over to *banks*. What you're seeing is the incestuous relationship between banking and government that will never go away, and that you need to bear boldly in mind when somebody complains that government isn't protecting them enough.

On government bailouts, Black said:

> [AIG] made bad loans. Their type of loan was to sell a guarantee, right? And they charged a lot of fees up front. So, they booked a lot of income, paid enormous bonuses. . . . and they got very, very rich. But, of course, then they had guaranteed this toxic waste, these liar's loans. Well, we've just gone through why those toxic waste, those liar's loans, are going to have enormous losses, and so you have to pay the guarantee on those enormous losses—and you go bankrupt. Except that you don't in the modern world, because you've come to the United States, and the taxpayers play the fool.

As government charged in with bailout money, failed bank CEOs kept their jobs. Why was that? To keep the cover-up in place. Honest people assigned as replacements would have immediately set out to find what went wrong, and government couldn't allow that. To keep the cover-up intact, CEOs who caused the problems were kept in place because they sure as heck weren't going to squeal.

Black showed that failed leaders were in cahoots with failed bankers. He said that, despite being one of the nation's top regulators during the subprime scandal, then–President of the Federal Reserve Bank of New York Timothy Geithner "took absolutely no effective action. He gave no warning. He did nothing in response to the FBI warning that there was an epidemic of fraud." Yet, he was responsible for regulating most of the large bank-holding companies in America.

Remember what you read earlier about government always promising after a crisis to clean things up with new regulations, then eventually ignoring the measures and allowing another crisis to unfold? Black is more familiar with that than almost anybody, because he's part of the team that put together just such measures after the savings and loan crisis only to see them ignored in the subprime mortgage crisis two decades later. He told Moyers:

> In the savings and loan debacle, we developed excellent ways for dealing with the frauds, and for dealing with the failed institutions. And for 15 years after the savings and loan crisis—didn't matter which party was in power—the U.S. Treasury secretary would fly over to Tokyo and tell the Japanese, "You ought to do things the way we did in the savings and loan crisis, because it worked really well. Instead you're covering up the bank losses because . . . you say you need confidence [and you] lie to the people to create confidence, and it doesn't work. You will cause your recession to continue and continue." The Japanese call it the lost decade. That was the result. So, now we get in trouble, and what do we do? We adopt the Japanese approach of lying about the assets.

Robert Rubin worked for 26 years at Goldman Sachs before becoming Treasury secretary under Bill Clinton. Rubin showed the ropes to Lawrence Summers, who then took over the Treasury for the last year and a half of the Clinton administration. Both Rubin and Summers worked to reduce and block regulations so banks could run wild, which eventually paved a primrose path to the subprime crisis.

Summers strongly backed two measures that, together, formed the plutonium core of the deregulatory A-bomb. The two measures were the Financial Services Modernization Act and the Commodity Futures Modernization Act, and by "modernization" they meant "meltdown." Let's look at each of the measures advocated by Summers.

The Financial Services Modernization Act smashed the wall created by the 1933 Glass-Steagall Act that had blocked any single company from combining in any way the services of investment banking, commercial banking, and insurance. That prevented companies from getting so big that they threatened the financial system, and it prevented the conflict of interest that arises when the same entity grants credit through lending and uses credit through investing. Glass-Steagall had worked like a charm for almost seven decades, then disappeared at the urging of Summers and others, most notably the banking lobby that had been trying to get around it for at least 20 years.

In opposition to the Act, North Dakota Democratic Senator Byron Dorgan said to the Senate in November 1999, ". . . we are, with this piece of legislation, moving towards greater risk. We are almost certainly moving towards substantial new concentration and mergers in the financial services industry, that is almost certainly not in the interests of consumers, and we are deliberately and certainly with this legislation moving towards inheriting much greater risk in our financial services industries. . . . I think we will, in ten years time, look back and say we should not have done that, because we forgot the lessons of the past." He was right.

Unfortunately, the Act passed. At the 1999 signing ceremony with President Clinton that saw the protections of Glass-Steagall fall away, Lawrence Summers called the new legislation "a major step forward to the twenty-first century," to which he probably should have added "and the eventual bankruptcy of our nation in a multitrillion-dollar giveaway of taxpayer money to banks that use this new deregulation to blow up the financial system." He left that last part out.

Summers is a real blessing to the country. Know what else you'll find on his resume? Having worked with bank lobbyists, Enron, and Republican Senator Phil Gramm to get through Congress the Commodity Futures Modernization Act, the prized piece of legislation that lit the fuse under the derivatives market time bomb by keeping it free of safety regulations. Brooksley Born served as chairperson of the Commodity Futures Trading Commission from summer 1996 to summer 1999, during which time she warned Congress that the exploding derivatives market "threatens our economy without any federal agency knowing about it." How did Summers handle her? By yelling at her on the phone. His team won, and Congress passed the law that barred her agency from doing anything as derivatives spun out of control. The subprime mortgage implosion proved her right and the Summers team wrong. She said in the March/April 2009 issue of *Stanford Magazine*:

> Recognizing the dangers . . . was not rocket science, but it was contrary to the conventional wisdom and certainly contrary to the economic interests of Wall Street at the moment. I certainly am not pleased with the results. I think the market grew so enormously, with so little oversight and regulation, that it made the financial crisis much deeper and more pervasive than it otherwise would have been.[3]

Thus utterly invalidated, Summers had seen his last days at the top, right? Don't be so sure. We'll come back to him in a moment.

As housing prices peaked in July 2006, another Goldman Sachs bankster, former CEO Henry Paulson, became Treasury secretary. Remember what you read earlier about the government bailing out AIG to protect its counterparties from their bad bets? We looked at a November 2009 report showing former New York Fed President Timothy Geithner following the guidelines written by the very banks that would benefit from the rescue. Right there working with him was Paulson, orchestrating the AIG bailout bonanza behind closed doors to benefit his former firm, Goldman Sachs, as recounted by Black:

> The Bush administration and now the Obama administration kept secret from us what was being done with

AIG. AIG was being used secretly to bail out favored banks like UBS and like Goldman Sachs, Secretary Paulson's firm [from which] he had come from being CEO. It got the largest amount of money, $12.9 billion, and they didn't want us to know that. . . . Paulson created a recommendation group to tell Treasury what they ought to do with AIG—and he put Goldman Sachs on it [even though the firm had a massive stake in the outcome]. Now, in most stages in American history, that would be a scandal of such proportions that he wouldn't be allowed in civilized society. . . . I don't know whether we've lost our capability of outrage, or whether the cover up has been so successful that people just don't have the facts to react to it.

It didn't even end there. Next, Paulson unveiled his rescue plan for the financial industry, the $700 billion bailout named the Troubled Asset Relief Program (TARP), which you saw in passing reference earlier. To administer the TARP funds, he appointed a Goldmanoid named Neel Kashkari. The funds were not intended for investment banks, so Goldman quickly changed itself from an investment bank to a bank holding company so it could get its share of the TARP. That gave it $10 billion cash from taxpayers, other emergency backing from taxpayers, and access to Federal Reserve lending. By the end of the first quarter of 2009, the Fed had lent or guaranteed almost $9 trillion in bailout program deals. To whom, you want to know? Ah, there's the rub. The Fed has the power to block congressional audits, so the exact amounts involved and the recipients are secret.

Luckily, Goldman and other culprits in the meltdown were finally brought under responsible government control, right? I'm afraid not. Once Goldman converted itself to a bank holding company, its overseer became the New York Fed. The chair of the New York Fed at that time was Stephen Friedman. Where do you suppose Friedman learned about the business of finance? Goldman, of course, where he once served as CEO. He was even on Goldman's board when regulation of the company became his official duty, which is a no-no. He received a conflict-of-interest waiver, and promptly bought another 52,000 shares of Goldman stock. Do you suppose he might possibly have regulated in a way that benefited his investment?

Once Obama came to town, though, things shaped up in a hurry, right? Well, no. In May 2009, Friedman took his millions and stepped down. Then, the person in charge of supervising Goldman became William Dudley. Finally, we had an independent third party—d'oh, wait a second, Dudley worked at Goldman from 1986 to 2007. He was the firm's chief economist just before Geithner hired him at the New York Fed to—don't laugh—"design numerous programs to try to guard the financial system against the worst crisis in generations," in the words of the *Washington Post*.[4] We saw how well those programs worked out.

At least you know who puts the gold in Goldman: *You* do, via taxes paid to the U.S. Treasury and then disbursed by former Goldman bigwigs who take turns running the Treasury. As of this writing in 2009, former Goldmanoids also run the World Bank and the New York Stock Exchange.

How was this possible even after a new administration arrived in January 2009 to finally clean things up? It was possible because there are no new administrations, just new names at the top to rearrange the same names lower on the org chart. Sure, a fresh day dawned in D.C., but President Obama appointed as his Treasury secretary . . . none other than Timothy Geithner, the man who failed to regulate banks as president of the New York Fed. Once a crony, always a crony. The Associated Press checked Geithner's phone records and found that most of his contacts with the financial sector in his first seven months as Treasury secretary were with only Citigroup, Goldman Sachs, and JP Morgan Chase. He learned his craft from former Treasury Secretary Robert Rubin the Goldman guy, and former Treasury Secretary Lawrence Summers, the protégé of

Rubin. They were the two who helped clear away financial regulations to let banks run wild. Whom did Obama choose as his economic adviser? That same Lawrence Summers.

Fine new line-up in Washington, eh? No wonder the financial crises just keep a-comin', age after age, and always will.

The Bummers of Summers

We have to give Lawrence Summers points for consistency, at least, even if it's consistent failure. After becoming Obama's National Economic Council director, Summers promised at the February 2009 signing of the $787-billion stimulus, called the American Recovery and Reinvestment Act of 2009, that it would prevent unemployment from exceeding 8.5 percent.

By November 2009, America had lost 3.4 million more jobs since February and the unemployment rate sat at 10.2 percent. What did Summers have to say about the situation? "I think we got the Recovery Act right." True to form.

Elected Officials Aren't the Real Leaders

If you want to know how hidebound Washington is, consider that it took only half a year for excitement over the new Obama administration to vaporize, once the allegedly angelic President Obama turned out to be a near clone of the reputedly reptilian President Bush. Not just in financial matters, either. It's worth studying the bigger picture of cronyism and corruption that defines government to better appreciate what a grip it has on your financial environment, too, so sit back and soak this up.

Obama won election partly by speaking out against lobbyists, that cabal of influence peddlers representing special interest groups whose special interests are usually not in anybody else's interest. To see their impact on Washington, let's go through some issues about which you're sure to have an opinion. For now, set aside your personal opinions and focus on how decisions about the issues get made.

Among lobbyists' proud accomplishments: keeping health care costs doubling every decade so that a greater percentage of stagnant incomes goes to insurance companies with each passing year; keeping Americans in gas-guzzling automobiles far beyond when electric cars became feasible; and keeping the U.S. military armed to the teeth with pet-contractor-built expensive weaponry that would prove devastating to the Third Reich, but is all but useless against modern enemies like terrorists. Candidate Obama assailed the "entire culture in Washington" that allows these kinds of things to happen. That culture has been great for health insurance companies and providers eager to expand profit margins to the point that 50 million Americans can't afford health care, oil companies wanting to sell every last barrel of crude before allowing a different energy source to take over, and military contractors happy to make billion-dollar weapon systems designed to destroy enemies that don't exist.

The Antilobbyist President Grows the Lobbying Corps

Candidate Obama vowed to pry lobbyist fingers from America's throat. In his June 2007 speech *Taking Our Government Back*, he looked at the beginning of the Industrial Revolution:

> From the politicians in Washington to the big city machines, a vast system of payoffs and patronage, scandal and corruption kept power in the hands of the few while the workers who streamed into the new factories found it harder and harder to earn a decent wage or work in a safe environment or get a day off once in awhile.

He praised Teddy Roosevelt's efforts to break up monopolies and bust trusts to give Americans a fair shot again, and said America requires that kind of leadership once more:

> We need a president who sees government not as a tool to enrich well-connected friends and high-priced lobbyists, but as the defender of fairness and opportunity for every American. That's what this country has always been about, and that's the kind of president I intend to be.

He was outraged:

> In the last six years, our leaders have thrown open the doors of Congress and the White House to an army of Washington lobbyists who have turned our government into a game only they can afford to play—a game played on a field that's no longer level, but rigged to always favor their own narrow agendas.

This would stop under him:

> But we need to clean up both ends of Pennsylvania Avenue. I believe that the responsibility for a people's politics begins with the person who sits in the Oval Office. That is why on my very first day as president, I will launch the most sweeping ethics reform in history to make the White House the people's house and send the Washington lobbyists back to K Street.

Too bad Candidate Obama and President Obama barely seemed to know each other. The former exited stage left as the latter entered stage right, to the sound of deafening applause. On January 21, 2009, his first full day in office, the new president stuck to his word by signing an executive order that banned the hiring of lobbyists to work in an issue area where they had lobbied in the previous two years. So far, so good. Shortly thereafter, the lobbying corps began to shrink, right?
Wrong.

That's what was supposed to happen, but didn't. Six months after Obama moved into the White House, the lobbying corps had *grown*, thanks to the president's many waivers to his own ban on hiring lobbyists, and a snowball of bailouts and new government initiatives. *The Hill* reported in July 2009 that special interest groups had "succeeded in slowing legislation to revamp the nation's health care system, won an essential change to climate change legislation, and put off efforts to set up a consumer agency in the financial sector."[5] Those who'd always been in charge remained in charge, and always will. They couldn't care less either whose name comes after the word "President" or which party name follows it.

Think I'm overstating the case? Look who Obama put in place as his deputy defense secretary, the second-most powerful position at the Pentagon: William Lynn, former top lobbyist for defense contractor Raytheon. You may have heard Raytheon's name yelled in protest against the invasion of Iraq, as it was widely criticized back then for encouraging military spending and profiting off wars. During Lynn's six years at Raytheon, the company spent almost $15 million lobbying politicians on projects like the Joint Standoff Weapon and sea-based missile defense. That was money well spent for the company, as those same six years saw Raytheon awarded more than $50 billion in general contracts, plus extra via subcontracts and group contracts. With supposedly antilobbyist Obama having appointed its former lobbyist as the Pentagon's number-two guy, Raytheon was positioned to do even better. I'm sure there's no connection, but anti-Iraq-war Obama made sure to ramp up the Afghanistan war as he ramped down the Iraq war. Gotta have a war somewhere, after all. Keeping the objectives vague and the timeline open-ended is the best approach. Tossing in a few bromides about defending freedom is a tried-and-true way to look heroic, because almost nobody stops to see if freedom is endangered. Same story, different map; same companies profiting, different people dying. What a difference a new president makes.

Every President Is an Oil Man

How about dependence on oil? In his campaign, Obama spoke out against the oil lobby. Here's what he said in one ad:

> Since the gas lines of the '70s, Democrats and Republicans have talked about energy independence, but nothing's changed—except now Exxon's making $40 billion a year, and we're paying $3.50 for gas. I'm Barack Obama. I don't take money from oil companies or Washington lobbyists, and I won't let them block change anymore. They'll pay a penalty on windfall profits. We'll invest in alternative energy, create jobs, and free ourselves from foreign oil. I approve this message because it's time that Washington worked for you, not them.

So pure, so fresh, so honest! "Finally," voters wet behind their political ears said, "we have a candidate who doesn't take money from oil companies." Unbeknownst to them, *no* presidential or congressional candidates do. Since the Tillman Act became law in 1907, corporations have been prohibited from contributing directly to federal candidates. They still buy candidates, of course, but for more than 100 years they've had to do so through political action committees and individual members of their companies. How much did Obama get from oil companies that way? According to the Center for Responsive Politics, $889,000. Viveca Novak and Justin Bank wrote at FactCheck.org in March 2008, "It's true that [Obama] doesn't accept contributions from individuals who are registered to lobby the federal government. But he does take money from their spouses and from other individuals at firms where lobbyists work. And some of his bigger fundraisers were registered lobbyists until they signed on with the Obama campaign."

People who heard Obama's campaign speeches and expected him to change America's energy picture received a quick Washington education. He proposed a cap-and-trade system in spring 2009 to limit carbon emissions, which seemed like a step in the right direction until the usual industry interests got hold of it. Among other efforts, they used what's called astroturfing. Astroturf is fake grass. Astroturf lobbying is fake grassroots, protests that look like they're coming from ordinary citizens when in fact they're organized by lobbying firms.

Newsweek reported in August 2009:

> In a memo leaked last week, oil industry lobbying organization the American Petroleum Institute asked regional companies to urge their employees to participate in planned protests (designed to appear independently organized) against the cap-and-trade legislation the House passed this summer. 'The objective of these rallies is to put a human face on the impacts of unsound energy policy and to aim a loud message at [20 different] states,' including Florida, Georgia, and Pennsylvania, wrote API president Jack Gerard. He went on to assure recipients of the memo that API will cover all organizational costs and handling of logistics.[6]

Those and other efforts by corporate interests worked, as captured by Jon Stewart's July 21, 2009, "Cap'n Trade" segment on *The Daily Show*:

> Kids, you want to see how a bill becomes a horribly compromised law? Well, let me introduce you to a friend of mine, Cap'n Trade. [Stewart speaks beside an image of Cap'n Trade as Superman, with bulging muscles, a red cape, and a blue suit.]
>
> He's the energy bill that was introduced in the House back in May. Super-strong! He's got one mission: to cut our carbon emissions by 20 percent by the year 2020. And by 20 percent, I mean 17 percent, which it was almost immediately dropped to. [Cap'n Trade's cape disappears.]

But he didn't need his cape, anyway, right? Anyway, Cap'n Trade is still going to make utilities get 25 percent of their energy from renewable resources by 2025. Or, he was, until that number was lowered to 15 percent by 2020 and states were given the option to make the number even lower, if they wanted to. [Cap'n Trade's muscles shrink so his arms and legs look like sticks.]

All right, well, he didn't need those muscles anyway. He's still Cap'n Trade! He can still charge polluters for 100 percent of their carbon credits . . . or get compromised into giving away 85 percent of those credits for free. [Cap'n Trade's pants fall down around his ankles.]

Yeah. Then, there were concessions that stripped the EPA of regulation authority over power plants, forestry, or agricultural firms. [Both of Cap'n Trade's eyes get blacked, and his left arm goes in a sling.]

Fifty million dollars was added for a national hurricane center in Congressman Grayson's district in Florida. [Cap'n Trade goes headfirst into a toilet.]

And another seemingly unrelated rider prevented the regulation of certain types of financial derivatives.

Take note of that last part about derivatives, as we'll come back to them later.

That's how things went against coal-burning carbon emitters. How about oil companies? Was Obama able to save the environment from their ways? No, he just moved the issue far away so fewer Americans would pay attention. In August 2009, the Obama administration agreed to lend $2 billion of U.S. taxpayer funds to Brazil's state-owned oil company, Petrobras, to support exploration of a large offshore discovery in the Tupi oil field near Rio de Janeiro. Candidate Obama had been fervently opposed to offshore drilling in Alaska, winning the support of environmentalists. With the Petrobras deal, President Obama angered that contingent by abandoning environmental concerns, continuing U.S. dependence on foreign oil, and funding in Brazil what he refused to fund at home. What's more, billionaire George Soros, who was an Obama backer in the campaign, just happened to have 49 percent of his portfolio in oil and gas stocks, with more than 22 percent in Petrobras alone. There's no connection, naturally, but it must have been a wonderful coincidence for Soros to see his primary stock holding propped up with U.S. tax dollars.

Every President Is a Banker

Remember Government Sucks, er, Goldman Sachs, the Wall Street bank that supplies presidents with Treasury secretaries? It plays a part in this discussion, too. President Obama appointed Tim Geithner as Treasury secretary, but he was merely trained by former Goldman bankster Robert Rubin and his protégé Lawrence Summers. That was a pretty good connection for Goldman, but apparently not good enough. Somebody brought it up with the new boss, and President Obama made a quick exception to his lobbyist-banning executive order and appointed former Goldman lobbyist Mark Patterson as Treasury Department chief of staff. On his first full day in office, Geithner announced rules to keep lobbyists away from allocating the rest of the bailout money in the Troubled Asset Relief Program, then introduced Patterson as the new chief of staff. There's a head-spinner for you. "These are the rules to keep lobbyists away from bailout money," Geithner seemed to say, "and now I'd like to introduce the new Treasury Department chief of staff, former Goldman Sachs lobbyist Mark Patterson." Huh?

Stuart Carlson suggested in a July 2009 political cartoon that Goldman Sachs change its name to Gold-In-Sacks. It showed two fat-cat bankers hauling bulging sacks of gold bigger than they are to a limousine. A skinny onlooker remarked to his friend, "Well, the name change *does* better reflect their current position. . . ."

Government of, by, and for the Corporations

In the Jon Stewart excerpt you read that the cap-and-trade bill intended to improve the environment by limiting carbon emissions contained a rider preventing the regulation of certain types of financial derivatives. Why would that be? What do financial derivatives have to do with carbon emissions? Leave it to Goldman Sachs to show you what, and to show how these seemingly unrelated examples we've been exploring are connected in a central place: government. It's where banks, corporations, and other special interest groups spend their money to get what they want, while voters naively study issues. To know what the future holds, just see who's paying for it.

In July 2009, Matt Taibbi wrote for *Rolling Stone*[7] a look at how Goldman has been manipulating markets and the economy since the Great Depression. He explained the company's formula, which it has used time and again:

> Goldman positions itself in the middle of a speculative bubble, selling investments they know are crap. Then they hoover up vast sums from the middle and lower floors of society with the aid of a crippled and corrupt state that allows it to rewrite the rules in exchange for the relative pennies the bank throws at political patronage. Finally, when it all goes bust, leaving millions of ordinary citizens broke and starving, they begin the entire process over again, riding in to rescue us all by lending us back our own money at interest, selling themselves as men above greed, just a bunch of really smart guys keeping the wheels greased. They've been pulling this same stunt over and over since the 1920s—and now they're preparing to do it again, creating what may be the biggest and most audacious bubble yet.[*]

The new bubble is made of those derivatives that magically found their way into the cap-and-trade bill to save the environment. More on those in a moment, but first let's

---

[*]Article by Matt Taibbi from *Rolling Stone*, July 9–23, 2009 © Rolling Stone LLC 2009.

look at Taibbi's exposé of government irrelevance in the face of big banking interests. Remember when oil and gas got so expensive back in 2008? Oil hit $147 per barrel that summer, in the midst of the presidential campaigns, and both sides missed the point. Here's Taibbi:

> In a classic example of how Republicans and Democrats respond to crises by engaging in fierce exchanges of moronic irrelevancies, John McCain insisted that ending the moratorium on offshore drilling would be "very helpful in the short term," while Barack Obama in typical liberal-arts yuppie style argued that federal investment in hybrid cars was the way out.

Unmentioned by both candidates was that the immediate supply of oil was fine, no shortage in sight. In fact, in the six months preceding the big price surge, supply was up and demand was down. That's supposed to lower prices, not raise them.

The reason prices rose is that speculators manipulated them, and of course Goldman led the effort. Taibbi wrote:

> Goldman did it by persuading pension funds and other large institutional investors to invest in oil futures—agreeing to buy oil at a certain price on a fixed date. The push transformed oil from a physical commodity, rigidly subject to supply and demand, into something to bet on, like a stock. Between 2003 and 2008, the amount of speculative money in commodities grew from $13 billion to $317 billion, an increase of 2,300 percent. By 2008, a barrel of oil was traded 27 times, on average, before it was actually delivered and consumed.

You may wonder why we don't have laws against such activities. In fact, we do, or did until 1991 when a Goldman subsidiary persuaded the Commodity Futures Trading Commission (CFTC) that Wall Street players needed the ability to hedge their positions against future price drops, just like farmers did. The concession to Goldman wasn't exactly trumpeted from rooftops. After interviewing people who were involved, such as former CFTC director of trading and markets Michael Greenberger, Taibbi concluded that the trading exemptions were "handed out more or less in secret." Then: "Armed with the semi-secret government exemption, Goldman had become the chief designer of a giant commodities betting parlor."

Boy, is it a big one, and better designed for Goldman than all the others it's overseen. At last, we see in Taibbi's words why derivatives were included in the cap-and-trade bill to save the environment:

> And instead of credit derivatives or oil futures or mortgage-backed CDOs, the new game in town, the next bubble, is in carbon credits—a booming trillion-dollar market that barely even exists yet, but will if the Democratic Party that [Goldman] gave $4,452,585 to in the last election manages to push into existence a groundbreaking new commodities bubble, disguised as an 'environmental plan,' called cap-and-trade.

Companies will buy and sell carbon allotments, and the market for them is expected to top $1 trillion. Goldman wants to own that market, so in 2008 it put up $3.5 million and placed its then-lobbyist Mark Patterson in charge of advocating on behalf of environmental regulations from government, a surprising new idea from a company as long opposed to government regulation as Goldman had been. Do you recognize the lobbyist's name? Yep, he's the same Mark Patterson who became Treasury Department chief of staff in the Obama administration.

This is one of the slickest moves yet made by a financial firm. Goldman gets more efficient with every passing president. In the old days under Clinton and Bush, Goldman had to wait for the government to collect taxes from the public and *then* pass them along to its corporate coffers. It won't need to mess with that interim step anymore because, as Taibbi explained, Goldman's version of cap-and-trade:

> . . . is really just a carbon tax structured so that private interests collect the revenues. Instead of simply imposing a fixed government levy on carbon pollution and forcing unclean energy producers to pay for the mess they make, cap-and-trade will allow a small tribe of greedy-as-hell Wall Street swine to turn yet another commodities market into a private tax collection scheme. This is worse than the bailout: It allows the bank to seize taxpayer money *before it's even collected.*

Where's government? Where's that team of irreproachable guardians you elected to represent you? They never did represent you. That's what we're seeing here. From the day you first knew their names, you knew all you needed to know: the names of the new people who'd be controlled by the real gang in charge.

Government immutability shows up in foreign policy, too. STRATFOR founder George Friedman wrote in August 2009 that "the single most remarkable thing about Obama's foreign policy is how consistent it is with the policies of former President George W. Bush."[8] Why? Because presidents "operate in the world of constraints; their options are limited." So much so in Friedman's view that he reminded everybody in February 2008, as the presidential campaigns heated up, that it wasn't terribly important who won because presidents "don't matter nearly as much as we would like to think and they would have us believe. Mostly, they are trapped in realities not of their own making." The country just gets batted around by events like terrorist attacks and financial meltdowns that somehow always produce lucrative contracts or bailouts or subsidies for special interest groups. On this, Peter Baker observed in the *New York Times* in February 2009, "Every four or eight years, a new president arrives in town, declares his determination to cleanse a dirty process and invariably winds up trying to reconcile the clear ideals of electioneering with the muddy business of governing."[9] Yet, somebody has to be the figurehead, so we go through the charade of change again and again.

If presidents as diametrically opposed as George W. Bush and Barack Obama produce the same political environments, is there any real hope for change? During the Obama campaign, the outlook for hope hit an all-time high when the outlook for lobbyists hit an all-time low. Six months after inauguration, they'd already switched positions. Rasmussen Reports showed in August 2009 that support for Obama hadn't just slipped, it had gone backwards to where most respondents disapproved of his performance as president. As lobbying profits soared, love for the president crashed.

Summer of the Lobbyist

To see why things stay the same, consider what boom times fell on lobbyist Heather Podesta as the economy slipped into the mud. The *Washington Post* profiled her in August 2009, describing her as "an It Girl in a new generation of young, highly connected, built-for-the-Obama-era lobbyists."[10] Wait a sec, I thought the Obama era was going to be all about fewer lobbyists. Why did I think that, again? Oh, that's right, because he said so during the campaign. Note to self: don't believe anything any of them say. Podesta told the *Post* that it was "a very good time to be a Democratic lobbyist," but, then again, "It's always a good time to be Heather Podesta." I guess so, because she's part of that same line of lever pullers that's been steadily backing citizens into a corner for ages. She married lobbyist Tony Podesta, brother of John Podesta, former President Bill Clinton's White House chief of staff and Obama's transition director. Elections don't change as many faces as people think. In the first half of 2009, Tony's lobbying firm grew 57 percent compared with the same period the year before. Heather's grew 65 percent. His shop collected $11.8 million in fees; hers collected $3.4 million.

Lobbying boom times hit such proportions that the *Post* dubbed summer 2009 the Summer of the Lobbyist, and Heather Podesta had her hands in each of the big three pots on the front burners with clients such as health insurance giants Cigna and HealthSouth, drugmaker Eli Lilly, financial outfits Prudential and Swiss Reinsurance, and Marathon Oil. Of course, boom times didn't come without sacrifices for the Podestas. Prior to the Obama lobbying extravaganza, they jetted off to their retreat in Venice 10 or 12 times per year but could make it only six times per year once their businesses began raking it in. Recessions affect everybody. We all get hit somehow.

The Center for Responsive Politics counts almost 25 lobbyists for every member of Congress. Each lobbyist helps various lawmakers raise campaign money, which puts the lawmakers in debt to the lobbyist, and that debt is repaid with the right vote or signature at the right time. The path of the money isn't hard to figure out: corporate interest to lobbying firm to lawmaker. That translates into whatever big business wants from government, big business gets from government. Sometimes it's the creation of a commodities trading system that will make tax collection a private endeavor benefiting a corporation, as Goldman Sachs arranged. Sometimes it's the handing over of cold cash from the Treasury to corporations, as the financial sector finagled. Citizens just vote and they think it matters which leader they choose, but all they're really doing is deciding between a kettle and a pot.

In Obama's June 2007 speech referenced earlier, the one where he promised to "launch the most sweeping ethics reform in history," he inadvertently made a spot-on forecast: "I know that in every campaign politicians make promises about cleaning up Washington. And most times, you end up disappointed when it doesn't happen. So it's easy to become cynical, to believe that change isn't possible; that the odds are too great; that this year is bound to be no different from the last." Then, Obama's first year in office was no different than Bush's last. Yes, it is easy to become cynical because it always goes that way. Replace "cynical" with "wise" and we may finally be getting somewhere. Anybody not cynical is either young, inattentive, or suffering from amnesia.

They Own Everything

The whole sham smacks of comedy, so it's fitting that one of the most perceptive summations of modern America came from a comedian, the late George Carlin. The following lightly edited excerpt is from his January 2006 HBO special *Life Is Worth Losing*:

> The big wealthy businessmen control things and make all the important decisions. Forget the politicians. They're irrelevant. The politicians are put there to give you the idea that you have freedom of choice.
>
> You don't.
>
> You have no choice. You have owners. They own you. They own everything. They own all the important land. They own and control the corporations. They've long since bought and paid for the Senate, the Congress, the state houses, the city halls, they've got the judges in their back pockets, and they own all the big media companies so they control just about all of the news and information you get to hear. They got you in a headlock. They spend billions of dollars every year lobbying to get what they want. Well, we know what they want. They want more for themselves and less for everybody else.
>
> But I'll tell you what they don't want. They don't want well-informed, well-educated people capable of critical thinking. They're not interested in that. That doesn't help them. That's against their interests. They don't want people who are smart enough to sit around the kitchen table to figure out how badly they're getting screwed by a system that threw them overboard

30 years ago. They don't want that. You know what they want? They want *obedient* workers. *Obedient* workers. People who are just smart enough to run the machines and do the paperwork, and just dumb enough to passively accept all these increasingly lousier jobs with the lower pay, the longer hours, the reduced benefits, the end of overtime, and the vanishing pension that disappears the minute you go to collect it—and now they're coming for your Social Security money. They want your retirement money. They want it back so they can give it to their criminal friends on Wall Street. And you know something? They'll get it. They'll get it all from you sooner or later because they own this place. It's a big club, and *you ain't in it.* You and I are not in the big club.

By the way, it's the same big club they use to beat you over the head with all day long when they tell you what to believe, all day long beating you over the head in their media telling you what to believe, what to think, and what to buy. The table is tilted, folks. The game is rigged. And nobody seems to notice. Nobody seems to care. Good, honest, hardworking people, white collar, blue collar—doesn't matter what color shirt you have on—good, honest, hardworking people continue— these are people of modest means—continue to elect these rich creeps who don't give a rip about them. They don't give a rip about you. They don't care about you—at all, at all, at all. . . . The owners of this country know the truth: it's called the American dream because you have to be asleep to believe it.

Carlin said this *before* the subprime crisis exposed these truths all over again. Collusion between government, banks, and business is nothing new. It existed before you were born, will be here your whole life, and will persist after you've passed on.

CHAPTER 6

How Money Is Power

The threats to your wealth rise like a cloud of money mosquitoes, even from parts of society outside the financial sector. Most areas of modern life are engineered in a way to get as much of your money as possible. Money is power. It buys influence that determines outcomes in favor of those who paid the money, and the outcomes they want give them more money. You've seen that in a few previous examples, and probably elsewhere in your life. Knowing what you're up against is the first step to protecting yourself against constant cash drainage.

Financial people are everywhere, and also financially stupid people are everywhere. Financial people occupy top positions in every industry behind every social issue and manipulate the cultural and legal environment so that more money from the population flows into fewer pockets at the top. Among the population, we find financially stupid people everywhere, focusing on the wrong issues and falling for the same tricks forever. The combination of financial people at the top and financially stupid people below has created the tilted table and rigged game that George Carlin talked about in the previous chapter, the four-flushing social contract of America in which nothing's quite as advertised.

Let's delve deeper into the nonfinancial-sector scenarios described in Chapter 5 to see if we can make educated guesses as to how they'll turn out. We'll look more closely at why health care is expensive, why oil dependency continues, and why military spending remains high. Each of these areas is costing you money—tons of money—and it's important to see what a coordinated effort is at work to suck dollars out of you.

You're sure to have a personal opinion on each issue, but try to set it aside for a moment to see the influence of corporate money on the decision-making process. That's all we're examining in these three scenarios. We'll touch upon political hair-triggers that raise emotions—triggers that special interests are expert at using to obscure the financial machinations at work. For now, pause your emotions and predispositions, and focus on the money flow.

Health Care Prices

Party A: People can't afford the medicine, health insurance, and medical services they need, so they ask government to do something to make health care more affordable.

Party B: Pharmaceutical companies, health insurance companies, and medical equipment manufacturers want as much profit as possible, so they ask government to maintain a system that keeps health care expensive.

A's Spending on Campaigns and Lobbying: $0

B's Spending on Campaigns and Lobbying: $1.3 billion

Would you say health care prices will get cheap or stay expensive? If you said "stay expensive," you win! If you added "probably forever," you get bonus points for perception, because every time Party A has to buy overly expensive health care from Party B, it helps to build the profit hoard that enables Party B to keep buying off politicians.

That's why a February 2009 report[1] from The Commonwealth Fund, which describes itself as "a private foundation working toward a high performance health system," found that, "The U.S. health care system is already the most expensive in the world, by far, and total health spending is projected to double by 2020—rising from a projected $2.6 trillion in 2009 to $5.2 trillion by 2020 to consume 21 percent of the nation's economic resources (gross domestic product)." It had been that way for a while. A July 2005 report[2] from The Commonwealth Fund found that "The latest data from the Organization for Economic Cooperation and Development (OECD), which compare trends among 30 industrialized countries, show that the U.S. spent $5,267 per capita on health care in 2002—53 percent more than any other country." Yet 50 million Americans have no coverage.

It's not just the price of medicine and services, it's the price of insurance, too. High insurance prices benefit private insurance companies, of course. Part of staying profitable involves cutting costs, which is why so many Americans find their insurance suddenly denied when the cost of their care gets too high. Health insurance companies are superb at keeping prices high and outlays low. The Securities and Exchange Commission (SEC) reported that between 2000 and 2007, health insurance profits rose 429 percent from $2.4 billion to $12.7 billion. The Census Bureau found that during those same years, the number of uninsured Americans grew 19 percent from 38.4 million to 45.7 million. In 2008, the number rose to 46.3 million. It's probably higher today due to rising unemployment in the recession, which is why I write that 50 million Americans are uninsured.

One proposed way to bring health care to all people instead of just those who can afford it is called single-payer insurance, where the single payer is a source managed by government to pay doctors and hospitals. It's the way Medicare works, with a focus on taking care of patients instead of taking care of corporate profits, but it's available only to people aged 65 and older. Under Medicare, none of the health care providers are government employees. The hospitals are private enterprises seeking a profit, but the health insurance is from the government and the government only. It's the single payer, and it loses none of its spending power to corporate inefficiencies, like a $12 million annual salary for the CEO, which is what the SEC reported to be the average pay for the CEOs of America's ten largest health insurance companies in 2007.

Most polls show the majority of Americans in support of single-payer insurance so that health care becomes a basic right of citizenship, as it is in most wealthy countries. Those opposed to it are, obviously, private insurance companies.

In a May 2009 survey,[3] The Commonwealth Fund found that "elderly Medicare beneficiaries reported greater overall satisfaction with their health coverage, better access to care, and fewer problems paying medical bills than people covered by employer-sponsored plans. The findings bolster the argument that offering a public insurance plan similar to Medicare to the under-65 population has the potential to improve access and reduce costs."

To me, this is common sense, and also happens to make good financial sense for everybody except insurance companies. All we're really discussing here is what kind of middle man works best to care for the health of the population. Why would you or I care who gives our money to the hospital when we get treatment? We just want the treatment. We can pay an insurance company first and have them pay for our treatment after the hospital fills out dozens of forms and we fight with our provider to prove that we actually needed the treatment—and lose about one-third of the total amount we pay to inefficiencies like the insurance company's profit. Or, we could redirect some of the money we already pay in taxes toward an American health insurance plan like Medicare, a single payer with an overhead one-tenth the amount eaten up by insurance companies, that requires no excessive paperwork at the hospital because everybody has the same national policy. Either way, we pay an insurance entity, and the entity pays the medical bill. With private insurance, we lose one-third of our spending power and have to fight a corporate bureaucracy to get treatment because the less treatment insurance companies approve the more they profit. With Medicare, we get maximum firepower from our money without having to fight because there's no profit motive at odds with our needs. If Medicare works so splendidly for people at 65, why wouldn't it work for people at 55, 45, 35, 25, and 15, too? Everybody needs better access and lower costs.

That's irrelevant, though, because discussions about any issue in America—certainly health care—are always about money for corporations, not about the issue. Those profiting off the current medical system outside of Medicare won't agree to any changes that could reduce their profits.

That's why, on the odds of ever making single-payer insurance like Medicare available to everybody in America, Vermont independent Senator Bernie Sanders said on *Ring of Fire Radio* in June 2009:

> I think the chances for a single-payer are going to be very, very difficult. We are going to have to mobilize people from one end of this country to the other end to begin to stand up for fundamental changes. But I got to tell you that the insurance companies, the drug companies, the medical equipment suppliers, they have spent hundreds and hundreds of millions of dollars in campaign contributions and lobbying in recent years, and it's going to be a tough, tough sledding to pass a single-payer, and it will even be difficult to pass a strong public option.[4]

Obama found that out the hard way. He said in a June 2003 speech to the AFL-CIO, when he was an Illinois state senator, that he'd like to see a single-payer health care plan, but that "we may not get there immediately, because first we have to take back the White House, we have to take back the Senate, and we have to take back the House." In his August 2008 acceptance speech at the Democratic Party's convention in Denver, he said he would "finally keep the promise of affordable, accessible health care for every single American."

Well, guess what? In 2009, his party had control of the White House, the Senate, and the House. It wasn't barely in control, either, but enjoyed a supermajority of 60 seats in the Senate. If ever Obama was in a position to put the health back in health care, it was then. Let's see how it went.

Death Panels and Socialism

People are so gullible that in summer 2009 some fell for the hogwash that health care reform included government "death panels" to review cases of elderly or disabled persons to decide if they should be allowed to live. There was no such provision, of course. The part of the proposal that corporate front groups spun into that fiction was the provision of "end-of-life counseling," where patients would be allowed funding to meet with their own doctors to discuss subjects such as living wills. It struck too few people as laughable that the health insurance companies responsible for denying coverage to people when it becomes too expensive suddenly grew concerned that the government would condemn people to die.

The death panel scare came from health care industry spokesperson Elizabeth "Betsy" McCaughey, who worked as a director for equipment maker Cantel Medical Corporation until resigning in August 2009 "to avoid any appearance of a conflict of interest during the national debate over health care reform," according to the press release. While still at Cantel, however, she said on *The Fred Thompson Show* on July 16, 2009, that the health care reform bill "would make it mandatory— absolutely required—that every five years people in Medicare have a required counseling session that will tell them how to end their life sooner, how to decline nutrition, how to decline being hydrated, how to go into hospice care. And by the way, the bill expressly says that if you get sick somewhere in that five-year period . . . you have to go through that session again, all to do what's in society's best interests or your family's best interests and cut your life short."[5]

The section she referred to was titled "Advance Care Planning Consultation," on page 425 of the bill. It did, indeed, show how Medicare would cover for the first time the cost of end-of-life counseling, and that "such consultation shall include the following: An explanation by the practitioner of advance care planning, including key questions and considerations, important steps, and suggested people to talk to; an explanation by the practitioner of advance directives, including living wills and durable powers of attorney, and their uses; an explanation by the practitioner of the role and responsibilities of a health care proxy."

Not a death panel in sight! No matter, the health care industry was off and running with another way to panic the populace into resisting changes that would save people a fortune in medical expenses. In August 2009, corporate opposition to health care pulled together an astroturf campaign to disrupt town hall meetings across America with death panel protesters. Recall from the previous discussion on corporate opposition to cap-and-trade that astroturfing is a lobbying technique that organizes people in a special interest group to look like ordinary citizens turning out to express their opinions. Such paid-for protests are actually fake grassroots, but few people realize that, so the protests gather momentum as bewildered nudniks pile on. That's why astroturfing remains an old favorite of lobbyists. It's a billion-dollar industry all by itself.

The death panel protesters, organized in the town hall astroturf campaign, turned what should have been a summer of careful discussion into a meaningless shouting match over false information. The health care industry laughed through it all, as profits appeared to be protected through yet another administration.

Their hero, Betsy McCaughey, had delivered for them again. Again? That's right. She wrote a cover story called "No Exit" for *The New Republic* against the Clinton health care reform plan in February 1994. One of her points back then was that if you weren't covered by a government health plan, you could not get treatment from a doctor even if you paid for it yourself. As with death panels in summer 2009, that claim was false. It didn't matter, though. The reason disinformation works is that people believe it. Say whatever you want people to fall for and a certain percentage of them will. It's fun; you should try it sometime. Despite the death panel red herring being such an obvious, easily disproved argument against health care reform, it gained traction while industry lobbyists doubled over with joy.

In addition to the death panel misinformation campaign, the health care industry pulled out some of its other tried-and-true techniques to keep health care private and profitable instead of public and affordable. One of those is referring to any kind of national health plan as socialist, and then deriding the very thought of allowing anything socialist in capitalist America. Yet, a quick glance around shows that government-run, socialist programs have been improving daily American life for ages: police departments, fire departments, schools, highways, Medicare, and the military are all socialist programs funded by taxpayers. In the case of Medicare, why should only some taxpayers get the benefits of national health insurance, and not others?

Corporations love socialism when it bails them out with billions of taxpayer dollars, but hate it when it uses tax-payer dollars to help taxpayers instead of fattening big business profits. Is the issue really socialism, or who's benefiting from the socialism? As you mull that over, note that the Congressional Budget Office reported that corporate income tax contributed only 12 percent of federal tax revenue in fiscal 2008.

One publication taking up the antisocialism fight against health care reform was *Investor's Business Daily*. It wanted to show that America was in danger of going the socialist way of the United Kingdom, which runs a popular publicly funded health care system called the National Health Service (NHS). The NHS is completely national, with the Department of Health owning hospitals, paying the salaries of doctors and other health care workers, and providing mostly free care to residents of the United Kingdom. In the United States, the Veterans Health Administration (VHA) operates in a similar manner but is available only to veterans, as you may have suspected from the name. *IBD* claimed that the United Kingdom's NHS was dangerous and would result in Americans dying if it were adopted in the United States, even though America's VHA cares for some eight million citizens at its nationwide network of more than 150 medical centers and boasts high customer satisfaction.

On July 31, 2009, *IBD* ran an editorial titled "How House Bill Runs Over Grandma"[6] in which it railed against the NHS, writing:

> The controlling of medical costs in countries such as Britain through rationing, and the health consequences thereof are legendary. The stories of people dying on a waiting list or being denied altogether read like a horror movie script. The U.K.'s National Institute for Health and Clinical Excellence (NICE) basically figures out who deserves treatment by using a cost-utility analysis based on the 'quality adjusted life year.' One year in perfect health gets you one point. Deductions are taken for blindness, for being in a wheelchair and so on. The more points you have, the more your life is considered worth saving, and the likelier you are to get care.

It made this outrageous, incorrect assertion:

> People such as scientist Stephen Hawking wouldn't have a chance in the U.K., where the National Health

Service would say the life of this brilliant man, because of his physical handicaps, is essentially worthless.

It proved inconvenient that Hawking, a theoretical physicist famous for his work on black holes and widely known for his best-selling book *A Brief History of Time*, was in fact born in the United Kingdom and lived there even as the paper went to press. In response to the editorial, Hawking, who is severely disabled and confined to a wheelchair by a motor neuron disease, told the *Daily Mail*, "I wouldn't be here today if it were not for the NHS. I have received a large amount of high quality treatment without which I would not have survived."

Ah, yes. The downside of disinformation is that it's disprovable, as the editors of *Investor's Business Daily* discovered. They couldn't possibly have chosen a worse example than Hawking. Not only was the scientist's life unthreatened by the U.K.'s National Health Service, he was alive *because* of it. As if to underscore how fortunate the world is for that fact, Hawking received the Presidential Medal of Freedom, the highest civilian honor in the United States, just two weeks after *IBD* ran its discredited editorial.

Cry Not For Hawking

If anybody is equipped to keep a big-picture perspective, it's a person who studies the universe. On his web site, Stephen Hawking wrote that he doesn't think much about his disability. "I try to lead as normal a life as possible, and not think about my condition, or regret the things it prevents me from doing, which are not that many."

He thinks that "physics can take one beyond one's limitations, like any other mental activity. The human race is so puny compared to the universe that being disabled is not of much cosmic significance."

Disinformation

Unfortunately, disinformation has been part of America's corporate health care game plan for a long time. In 2006, AARP, the nonpartisan group for people age 50 and over, looked into who was behind some of the health care disinformation going to elderly Americans. Bill Hogan wrote in *AARP Bulletin Today*[7] about three groups: United Seniors Association, The Seniors Coalition, and the 60 Plus Association. "More than ever before, they've been trying to influence political campaigns and shape policies that affect older Americans," he found. "But who's really behind these organizations? And are they really working to help older Americans?"

Come to find out, the pharmaceutical industry bankrolled all three. To defeat prescription drug legislation at the state level, it used the 60 Plus Association as its front group. Hogan wrote, "Among other things, it hired Bonner & Associates, a Washington-based firm that specializes in 'Astroturf lobbying'—so named because it's the 'artificial' version of grassroots lobbying—to fight such legislation in Minnesota and New Mexico. The firm's paid callers, reading from scripts that identified them as representatives of 60 Plus, urged residents to ask their governors to veto the legislation. Pharmaceutical giant Pfizer, Inc., later said it had paid Bonner & Associates to make the calls."

Frank Clemente, the director of Public Citizen's Congress Watch, told Hogan, "I think of the pharmaceutical industry as being like an octopus, with a deep reach no other industry can match. This is an industry that's not only spending more on direct lobbying than any other industry but also spending more on front groups and related entities than any other industry."

Right there with it is the health insurance industry. Its lobby, America's Health Insurance Plans (AHIP), panicked in summer 2009 when Congress began discussing a Medicare-like program for all citizens. As you know by now, such a program's low costs would have forced private insurance companies to cut back on profits to remain competitive. Why, it could have even forced more money into caring for policy holders instead of paying executive bonuses and fueling corporate jets, a change of plan that was simply unacceptable. So, AHIP contributed to the astroturf campaign by organizing some 50,000 employees of the insurance industry to storm town hall meetings and oppose any public plan.

Preexisting Condition

The following excerpt comes from the October 28, 2009, episode of *The Colbert Report*, with Stephen Colbert.

The fact is, folks, we *all* have something. Maybe you've got a flawed aorta that didn't show up on the EKG, or a genetic predisposition for horking down bacon. For insurance companies, we might as well be subprime mortgages. So, I say, don't blame the insurers, folks. . . .

So, if insurance companies are going to cover all people, first we're going to have to start making people without preexisting conditions, by breeding the insurable with the insurable. . . . Now, remember folks, selective breeding and genetic modification have worked miracles for our fruits, vegetables, and livestock.

So, if you are a healthy woman who qualifies for insurance, let's mate you with one of the few men we know an insurance company would never deny coverage to: their CEO. Your baby will never be denied coverage for being too fat or too skinny if you mate with Rocky Mountain Health Plan CEO Steve ErkenBrack. He makes those babies just right. And, ladies, don't worry about being denied coverage after your C-section if that baby got planted by Golden Rule Health CEO Richard A. Collins.

Now, some people may find it unpleasant to have their loved ones screwed by insurance CEOs but, face it, that is our present preexisting condition.

A separate lobbyist-run group opposed to health care reform, FreedomWorks, circulated among its members a memo[8] titled, "Rocking the Town Halls—Best Practices," which included "Artificially Inflate Your Numbers," "Be Disruptive Early and Often," and "Try To 'Rattle Him,' Not Have an Intelligent Debate." That last one's a good point, because heaven knows the last thing we need when trying to craft an affordable health care system is any kind of intelligent debate. Two-word slogans like "No Socialism!" are a much better approach.

When watching footage of the people that turned up at town hall meetings to oppose health care, I couldn't help but notice how many of them looked in need of precisely what a single-payer system would provide. The young ones looked a little short on cash and the old ones, well, they were covered by the Medicare single-payer system. The protesters were taught to believe that health care reform means socialism and a liberal takeover. You can bet that corporations profiting off the current health care system loved that.

"Leave us alone," health industry corporations cried. "Let us be good capitalists. The business of America is business!" Meanwhile, people's signs at the protests should have read "Keep our money going to corporations, not health care!" or "More money for corporations so they can pay lobbyists to buy off politicians so Americans can't get health care! Yea!"

Instead of seeing the flow of money and how they were being used as rubes again, the astroturf-duped throngs did exactly what corporations wanted them to do: protested in favor of company profits. How many cigars were smoked in corporate headquarters while that footage played on TV? No wonder people fall farther behind in their finances every year. They beg to do so.

We Prefer Sick People

Dr. Andrew Weil, author of several books on health, including *Why Our Health Matters: A Vision of Medicine That Can*

Transform Our Future, appeared on *Larry King Live*[9] in September 2009. Regarding health care costs, he said:

> We spend more per capita on health care than any people in the world, and we have very little to show for it. Our health outcomes are dismal. We've been paying more and more, and getting less and less for it, and if we don't do something about this it will sink us economically. We'll be spending up to 20 percent of our gross domestic product on health care, and we can't sustain that. It will make us bankrupt.

He said that the real way to get costs down is "to shift our efforts toward prevention" and "change the nature of medicine." He touched on a key failing of our system that relies upon medical corporations obsessed with swelling profits: it wants more sick people. Think about it. When a company makes money selling cures, it wants ailments. Taking special note of all the ways that the corporate profit motive gets in the way of care, look at Weil's plan:

> First of all, we don't have a health care system in this country. We have a disease management system that's horribly dysfunctional and getting worse by the day, and the vast majority of disease that we're trying to manage is lifestyle related and therefore preventable. So, what we really need to do is to shift our energies away from disease management toward making people healthy and preventing them from getting sick.
>
> Secondly, the kinds of interventions that we're using to treat disease are way too expensive because they're dependent on technology—I include pharmaceuticals in that. We need a new kind of medicine in which doctors know how [to practice], and patients accept: low-tech, high-touch approaches to the treatment of illness.
>
> I would immediately ban direct-to-consumer advertising of pharmaceutical drugs. That's been a disaster

for patients and doctors, and a great boon to the drug companies. No other country in the world allows that, except New Zealand. Stop that right away.

I'd set up an office of health education in the Department of Education with adequate funds to get serious about K-through-12 health education, starting with teaching kids about what health is and what life-style choices promote it. . . . The meat of prevention is about teaching people how to make the right choices about food, how to keep your body physically active, how to deal with stress. We have to change a whole philosophy!

Our priorities of reimbursement are completely backward. We don't pay for preventive strategies, we pay for intervention.

As the economic crisis in health care deepens, which it certainly will, it's going to force this deeper kind of change. At the moment, all I hear about is how we're going to give more people access to the present system and how we're going to pay for it. To me, that's not the issue. The present system doesn't work, and it's going to take us down. We need a whole new kind of medicine.

More accurately, the present system doesn't work for the health of citizens but works beautifully for the profits of corporations. The last thing corporate health care wants is a population educated in the tenets of healthy living. Healthy people don't run up high medical bills. Sick people do. Small wonder, then, that society is geared toward fixing sick people instead of making healthy people.

There's an exception to that, but it won't make you very happy. Health insurance companies prefer healthy people because such customers pay for policies that are not needed. When policyholders get too sick and expensive, insurance companies look for ways to drop them, which is called rescission, as in "We rescind your policy."

Lovely. The only companies in the health industry who want healthy people are the insurance companies so they don't have to pay for care. Beyond them, pharmaceutical outfits and medical device makers and other providers of care prefer sick people, because they become customers.

The pattern holds. Companies win; citizens lose.

Naming the Cure

One problem with passing a national health insurance plan is naming it. Terms used in 2009 included public option and government insurance. Neither appealed to anybody and both made it easy for opponents to scream "socialism!" at proposals. Those trying to create national health insurance in the future should meet with a marketing firm first. Something along the lines of Americare or Healthy America could work.

To get the ideas flowing, here are some other suggestions: Capital Condition, Department of Vim and Vigor, Federal Fine Fettle, Hale and Hearty Homeland, Here I Am Uncle Sam, Internal Vitality Service, Live Another Day U.S.A., Medicare For Me, No Patient Left Behind, No-Pauper Palliative, Salubrious and Solvent, Something Gone Right, Tax and Mend, Tip Top from Taxes, and Washington Wellness.

The Wall Street–Run Insurance Plan

One guy who knows a thing or two about the ways of health insurance companies is Wendell Potter, a former vice president of corporate communications at health insurance giant Cigna. He became a whistleblower when he saw a Remote Area Medical operation in rural Virginia in July 2007. Remote Area Medical was founded in 1985 to bring medical services to people in Third World countries, but began running operations in the United States as the number of Americans without health coverage grew over the years. That day in Virginia, Potter saw long lines of people without medical insurance waiting in the rain to receive free basic care. Some of them had driven hundreds of miles. Their treatment happened outdoors in broad daylight, or in animal stalls at the county fairgrounds. Two years later, Potter recalled to *The Observer*, "It was overpowering. It was just more than I could possibly have imagined could be happening in America." He quit his job at Cigna soon after witnessing the Remote Area Medical operation.

In June 2009, Potter testified before the U.S. Senate Committee on Commerce, Science, and Transportation. From his testimony:

> Insurers make promises they have no intention of keeping, they flout regulations designed to protect consumers, and they make it nearly impossible to understand—or even to obtain—information we need. As you hold hearings and discuss legislative proposals over the coming weeks, I encourage you to look very closely at the role for-profit insurance companies play in making our health care system both the most expensive and one of the most dysfunctional in the world.
>
> When I left my job as head of corporate communications for one of the country's largest insurers, I did not intend to go public as a former insider. However, it recently became abundantly clear to me that the industry's charm offensive—which is the most visible part of duplicitous and well-financed PR and lobbying campaigns—may well shape reform in a way that benefits Wall Street far more than average Americans.
>
> To help meet Wall Street's relentless profit expectations, insurers routinely dump policyholders who are less profitable or who get sick. Insurers have several ways to cull the sick from their rolls. One is policy rescission. They look carefully to see if a sick policyholder may have omitted a minor illness, a preexisting condition, when applying for coverage, and then they use that as justification to cancel the policy, even if the enrollee has never missed a premium payment.

Americans need and overwhelmingly support the option of obtaining coverage from a public plan. The industry and its backers are using fear tactics, as they did in 1994, to tar a transparent, publicly accountable health care option as a "government-run system." But what we have today, Mr. Chairman, is a Wall Street–run system that has proven itself an untrustworthy partner to its customers, to the doctors and hospitals who deliver care, and to the state and federal governments that attempt to regulate it.[10]

If you have to sit down, I'll understand. How shocking that Wall Street, that assembly of do-rights always looking out for the public good, puts health care profits ahead of health care care. This theme repeats, so identify the pattern in your mind for easy recognition later. Companies profit with policies that are good for them, not you, and they spend ungodly sums of money to create a legal environment that enables them to do so. You thought health care was about health. It's not in America, hasn't been for decades. It's about money.

"Hold on," you say. "I thought Obama pledged to do something about that." Indeed he did and indeed he tried, just as Clinton tried in 1994, Nixon tried in 1974, and Truman tried in 1945. You know now how each administration fared against health care's corporate interest groups. Then again, you knew back at the very beginning of this section how they'd fare by just looking at how much money the health care industry spends on campaigns and lobbying. Over the past seven decades, health care expenses as a percentage of America's gross domestic product have grown, while the ranks of uninsured Americans have swelled.

In the October 9, 2009, episode of *Bill Moyers Journal*, Moyers discussed the health insurance lobby's grip on the Senate Finance Committee, chaired by Montana Democratic Senator Max Baucus. Moyers showed a video of Baucus speaking, and told viewers to "take a close look at that woman sitting behind" Baucus. Moyers continued:

> She used to work for WellPoint, the largest health insurer in the country. She was Vice President of Public Policy, and now she's working for the very committee with the most power to give her old company and the entire industry exactly what they want: higher profits, and no competition from alternative nonprofit coverage that could lower costs and premiums.
>
> I'm not making this up. Here's another little eye-opener. The woman who was Baucus's top health advisor before he hired Liz Fowler? Her name is Michelle Easton. Why did she leave the committee? To go to work—where else?—at a firm representing the same company Liz Fowler worked for: WellPoint. As a lobbyist.
>
> It's the old Washington shell game. Lobbyist out, lobbyist in. And it's why they always win.[11]

Moyers reported that the members of the Senate Finance Committee had "collected nearly 50 million dollars from the health sector, a long-term investment that's now paying off like a busted slot machine."

Health Care Reform's Prognosis

At this book's publishing deadline, the health care reform effort wasn't yet finished. It was far enough along, however, for me to make an educated guess on how it would turn out. When you read this, check to see how close my prognosis came to the final result.

Before we look, though, ask yourself what you'd want to have happen if you were a health industry corporation trying to protect your fat profit margin through a reform attempt. Would you want reform in a way that shrank your profit? No. Then again, would you want to be known as a bloodless company that blocked a plan to extend medical coverage to millions of Americans? No. The best outcome for you would be some kind of health care reform that would make people happy, but leave your profits intact or, better yet, grow them. If you could make more money off the reformed health care system, you'd be sitting pretty because you'd finally be off the list of America's most evil corporations, but getting even richer than before. If that outcome looked best to health industry corporations, don't you suppose it was the most likely? Of course.

The House passed its version of a reform bill by a tiny five-vote margin, 220–215, on November 7, 2009. You'd think the closeness of the vote betrayed a revolutionary change in the offing, with almost half the House opposed to radical departure from the status quo. Wrong. It was reform that only corporations could love.

The House bill, H.R. 3962, made no progress toward ending for-profit health insurance. Instead, it sent more dollars to insurance companies by requiring some 21 million Americans to buy private health insurance from the existing gang of corporations that have driven up the cost of care by *not* paying people's medical bills. The new requirement added more than $70 billion to the health insurance industry's annual revenue, much of which was to be funded by taxpayers. On this point, Ohio Democratic Congressman Dennis Kucinich said in a statement issued on November 7, 2009, explaining why he voted no, "This inevitably will lead to even more costs, more subsidies, and higher profits for insurance companies—a bailout under a blue cross." He continued:

> By incurring only a new requirement to cover preexisting conditions, a weakened public option, and a few other important but limited concessions, the health insurance companies are getting quite a deal. . . .
>
> During the debate, when the interests of insurance companies would have been effectively challenged, that

challenge was turned back. The "robust public option" which would have offered a modicum of competition to a monopolistic industry was whittled down from an initial potential enrollment of 129 million Americans to 6 million. An amendment which would have protected the rights of states to pursue single-payer health care was stripped from the bill at the request of the Administration. . . .

This health care bill continues the redistribution of wealth to Wall Street. . . .[12]

If anything passes at all, it will be the same variety of change we're always sold in politics: fun, but ultimately meaningless. Health care reform in 2009 offered a big chance to get something right, but was wasted—again.

The list of potential solutions included:

- A fully national system like the United Kingdom's National Health Service or America's Veteran's Health Administration, in which the country owns the hospitals and employs the doctors and staff. Under such a program every citizen would be entitled to free health care funded by taxes, and costs would be directly controlled.
- A single-payer system like the national health insurance of Canada and America's Medicare system, in which the country provides every citizen with health insurance that they use at privately owned hospitals. Under such a program, costs would be indirectly controlled by the pay limits established by the insurance.
- A national health insurance that competes with private insurers and covers people that the private industry turns away. This was the so-called public option in the debates of 2009. In its strongest version, every citizen would be able to choose the public option.
- A watered-down public option available only to people who do not already have private insurance. If a person

was covered by private insurance, they would not be eligible for the public option even if that option was cheaper.

- A more watered-down public option would limit the option to certain states only.
- An even more watered-down public option, called the triggered public option, would become available only after private insurance companies failed to make health insurance affordable within four or five years.

In that spectrum from total coverage to basically the status quo, where did the legislation fall? In the watered-down region, naturally, leaning toward a public option available to some people in some places. As the discussion moved from the House to the Senate, even that looked ready to break down further into the triggered public option.

No Public Option at All

This just in! I had one last chance to sneak something into the book in January 2010, and was amused to see the predictions of this section already coming true. The public option fell from even the watered-down region of the spectrum of choices to disappear entirely. Poof! There went health care reform—again. From the January 4–11, 2010, issue of *The Weekly Standard*:

> The goal was to get a large swath of the public insured by the government, and so gradually create a socialized insurance system. . . .
>
> But in order to gain 60 votes in the Senate, the Democrats have now had to give up, for all practical purposes, on any version of that public insurer, while leaving the other components of their scheme in place. The result makes no sense whatsoever—not to conservatives, not to liberals, not to anyone. Rather

than reform a system that everyone agrees is a failure, it will subsidize that system and compel participation in it—requiring all Americans to pay ever-growing premiums to private insurance companies, most of which are for-profit, while doing essentially nothing about the underlying causes of those rising costs. The thought that, after all of this, a Democratic Congress is going to force Americans to send their premiums to the despised insurance industry and then subsidize that industry to boot has sent the left into such a state of frenzied recriminations it could sink the whole enterprise yet."

Source: James C. Capretta and Levin, Yuval, "A Fine Mess," *Weekly Standard*, January 4-11, 2010, www.weeklystandard.com/Content/Public/Articles/000/000/017/389uruts.asp.

Some kind of reform will have probably passed between the time I wrote this and the time you're reading it, but that something won't mean much. To see how much it means to you, ask yourself two questions: "Has the cost of my health care come down?" and "Have my taxes come down?" If the answer to each is no, then the health care reform effort meant nothing to you. That's the most likely situation. Another possibility of meaningless reform would be lower health care costs, but higher taxes that either offset or exceed your health care savings.

Remember, The Commonwealth Fund projects that more than one-fifth of the nation's economic resources will be used for health care spending by 2020. That represents a doubling from current levels, which are already the most expensive in the world.

What's even more galling is that the cost of the proposed meaningful U.S. health care reform of 2009 was $1 trillion over 10 years, or about $100 billion per year.

What's That Date, Again?

The following extract is from President Nixon's special message to Congress proposing a national health insurance plan, delivered February 6, 1974:

> ... (T)he overall cost of health care has still risen by more than 20 percent in the last two and one-half years, so that more and more Americans face staggering bills when they receive medical help today. . . . For the average family, it is clear that without adequate insurance, even normal care can be a financial burden, while a catastrophic illness can mean catastrophic debt.
>
> Beyond the question of the prices of health care, our present system of health care insurance suffers from two major flaws.
>
> First, even though more Americans carry health insurance than ever before, the 25 million Americans who remain uninsured often need it the most and are most unlikely to obtain it. . . . Second, those Americans who do carry health insurance often lack coverage which is balanced, comprehensive, and fully protective.
>
> Comprehensive health insurance is an idea whose time has come in America.
>
> There has long been a need to assure every American financial access to high quality health care. As medical costs go up, that need grows more pressing.
>
> Now, for the first time, we have not just the need but the will to get this job done. There is widespread support in the Congress and in the Nation for some form of comprehensive health insurance.
>
> Surely if we have the will, 1974 should also be the year that we find the way.

Do you remember how much TARP, the government handover of taxpayer dollars to the big banks that blew up the financial system, cost taxpayers? $700 billion. Health care reform slated to cost $100 billion annually and bring coverage to every citizen was fomented into a national brawl with astro-turf protests against fictions like death panels. A $700-billion transfer of taxpayer wealth to banking tycoons was barely even discussed, much less protested. In both cases, corporations got what they wanted; citizens got screwed.

The Center for Responsive Politics reports that the health sector paid $828 million to campaigns from 1990 to 2008, and in 2008 alone they spent almost $500 million for the services of 3,000 lobbyists. They pay to keep health care spending high, so that's where it will stay.

Let's try another one.

Oil Dependency

Party A: People are tired of using oil for transportation. Gasoline is expensive; exhaust from internal combustion engines is bad for the environment; stopping at gas stations is inconvenient; electric motors are quieter, cleaner, and have more power; and depending on foreign oil is bad for national security because: one, it provides terrorist-sponsoring countries with money to pay for terrorist activities and, two, it leaves the United States vulnerable to oil supply disruptions. People want automobiles that don't use oil.

Party B: Oil and gas companies make more money than any other companies on the planet, and they do so by keeping people dependent on oil. Estimates vary, but the world has about one trillion barrels of oil left in its proven reserves. At $100 per barrel, that represents $100 trillion of sales left in the oil business. To get all of it, oil companies want to keep people in automobiles that use oil until every barrel is pumped and sold.

A's Spending on Campaigns and Lobbying: $0

B's Spending on Campaigns and Lobbying: $368 million

Do you think automobiles will stop using oil? If you said "no," you win! By keeping alive the misperception that alternative technologies are futuristic, the oil industry has preserved gasoline as the only way to power your automobile.

According to an April 2009 report[13] in *Forbes*, the world's five largest companies by sales volume were:

- Royal Dutch Shell, with $458 billion
- ExxonMobil, with $426 billion
- Wal-Mart Stores, with $406 billion
- BP, with $361 billion
- Toyota Motor, with $263 billion

When judged by sales, oil companies account for three of the top five, and six of the top 10. When judged by earnings, which are sales minus expenses such as the cost of goods sold, the result is even more lopsided toward oil companies:

- ExxonMobil, with $45 billion
- Gazprom, with $27 billion
- Royal Dutch Shell, with $26 billion
- Chevron, with $24 billion
- BP, with $21 billion

Yes, every one of the world's five most profitable companies is in the oil business. Chevron and ExxonMobil are based in the United States, Gazprom is based in Russia, Shell is based in the Netherlands, and BP is based in the United Kingdom. Among the world's 50 most profitable companies, *Forbes* also counted oil outfits in Brazil, China, France, and Italy. It's the biggest business on Earth, and it's everywhere on Earth.

The American Council for Energy-Efficient Economy (ACEEE) estimates that some 90 percent of the greenhouse gas emissions produced by a vehicle are created by burning gasoline. On top of that, the Union of Concerned Scientists says that oil-fueled transportation is the biggest air polluter in the United States. Yet, more than 95 percent of automobiles on America's roads still run on gasoline.

Is that because of limitations in other technologies? That's what people have been told, with talk of electric cars being a vision of the future. They're actually a legacy of the past. They were invented in the 1800s alongside gasoline cars, and they outsold gasoline cars in the early 1900s. One hundred years ago, more Americans drove electric cars than drove gasoline cars. Even gas-electric hybrids are old news, not futuristic. It was 1905 when American engineer H. Piper filed a patent for his hybrid gas-electric engine that would deliver acceleration from zero to 25 miles per hour in 10 seconds. All it takes is a trip to any distribution center to see a fleet of electric vehicles (EVs) hard at work right now. You didn't think forklifts burned gasoline inside the closed quarters of a warehouse, did you? No, electric models have been available for more than 80 years. Golf courses, too, show that EVs are practical, and transporting people every day. I'm not suggesting that we drive around in forklifts and golf carts, of course, but their presence shows that electric propulsion is ready for work right now.

What changed to get Americans behind the wheels of gasoline cars instead of electric? Oil was discovered in the 1920s in California, Oklahoma, and Texas. Better, longer roads favored faster cars with greater driving ranges, and gasoline was better than electric on both fronts at that time. Henry Ford's mass production techniques dropped the price of gasoline cars dramatically in 1915, to less than $10,000 in today's money, while electric models cost almost $40,000. We can point to technology as the reason gasoline won out in the early years of automotive transportation. We cannot point to it as the reason gasoline has remained the only choice for a century.

Seeing his fleet of electric forklifts in action led a business owner friend of mine in Los Angeles to wonder why he couldn't buy a regular car that operated in the same way. Then, General Motors released its EV1 in Los Angeles and he leased one in 1998, and let me drive it around town one day. It was quiet, did everything I needed, and went 75 miles on a charge. My friend said that on rare occasions when he needed to drive more than 75 miles in a day, he'd take a gasoline-powered car. He wouldn't have to do that now because new batteries hold a charge longer.

The appeal of clean electric propulsion filled long waiting lists of consumers wanting to buy the EV1, but General Motors mysteriously yanked it from the market. It said there was too little demand, and even commissioned a study that concluded people would choose electric cars only if they cost $28,000 less than comparable gasoline cars. That was a little hard to believe when the electric version of Toyota's RAV4 packed a waiting list of its own in 2003, despite costing $30,000. It recharged in five hours and could go about 100 miles per charge. Its top speed was 78 miles per hour. Waiting lists notwithstanding, Toyota mysteriously yanked the RAV4-EV from the market.

The companies shouldn't have been surprised by the waiting lists. In 2000, in response to GM's study showing little demand for electric vehicles, the California Electric Transportation Coalition (CalETC) conducted its own survey,[14] using what Executive Director David Modisette described as "the same research methodologies employed by the auto industry to identify markets for its gasoline vehicles." The study found that between 12 and 18 percent of California car shoppers in the light-duty segment would buy an electric vehicle. That translated into an annual sales potential in the range of 150,000 to 230,000 vehicles. Half of the 934 new-car buyers surveyed said they would accept a per-charge range of 60 to 80 miles. A third of the group said they'd buy an electric vehicle as their next car if it cost about the same as a gasoline-powered model. Modisette said, "This is the study the auto industry didn't want to see. . . . The results show there is a very strong consumer market for EVs in California, a demand automakers either don't want to believe or want to go away."

Seeing such surveys always makes me throw my hands up and think, "Of course! Who would *not* go for an electric car if it was big enough, fast enough, went far enough, and recharged easily? What's to prefer about gasoline power?" It's like reading a survey that says most respondents prefer a razor that does *not* cut them while shaving. Me, too! On the electric vehicle idea, I'd like to park in my garage, pull a plug from the hood of the car to a wall outlet, and let it recharge while I'm home. Wouldn't you? There'd be no more annoying and *expensive* stops at gas stations, no more exhaust smells, no more loud noise from under the hood. From the get-go, the auto industry's claim that there wasn't enough demand for electric vehicles looked fishy.

Why would car companies care what kinds of cars they sell, as long as people buy them? One reason for the resistance to electric vehicles could be that electric cars are more efficient and use fewer parts that wear out, which means repair and maintenance profits would drop. Still, a runaway successful electric car program would have plenty of opportunities to build in add-on services, customizations, battery upgrades, and so on. No, it seems there had to have been a different pressure to leave the electric car technology on the same shelf where it's been ignored for a century.

With nobody talking, it's hard to connect the dots to make an airtight case for where that pressure may have come from, but we can at least put a few dots on the page.

Oil companies lobbied hard against California's Zero Emission Vehicle (ZEV) Mandate, which the state drafted in response to rising ozone levels in the Los Angeles area that triggered 41 stage-one smog alerts in 1990. The California Air Resources Board required that 10 percent of new vehicles sold in California be emission-free by 2003. That set off alarm bells in oil offices across the nation.

In a January 2005 FEEM working paper titled *The Allure of Technology: How France and California Promoted Electric Vehicles to Reduce Urban Air Pollution*,[15] authors David Calef of FEEM and Robert Goble of Clark University wrote,

"Perceiving the appearance of EVs as a direct threat to their monopoly on fuels for automobiles, the oil companies were bluntly hostile to the ZEV mandate while the major automakers were at best reluctant to reconfigure their industry around electric motors powered by rechargeable batteries."

Use less oil? "No, no, no," said the oil industry. They reached into their well-worn file cabinet to get out the same playbook that's always worked for them. Calef and Goble continue: "The oil companies employed a traditional method of influencing public policy formulation by contributing money to candidates for political office. Atlantic Richfield Co., BP America, Exxon, Mobil Oil Co., Phillips Petroleum, Shell Oil Co., and Texaco donated a total of $1.1 million to legislative candidates in 1994 and in the first six months of 1995." California's governor at that time, Pete Wilson, received $325,000 from oil industry groups.

Mobil Oil devised a particularly effective strategy that sought to create skepticism around electric cars and other alternative fuel vehicles. It spent more than $3 million buying recurring ad space in the *New York Times, USA Today*, the *Wall Street Journal,* and the *Washington Post* along with popular magazines like *Newsweek* and *Time*. According to Calef and Goble, the campaign had three goals:

1. Reassure people that the world was not running out of oil.
2. Illustrate the inadequacy of EV technology as a means of transportation for the average American, and discredit their environmental benefits.
3. Foster the values of the free-market system, which Mobil saw as threatened by ever-expanding government regulations, and stir up economic apprehension by arguing that the mandate would cause tax increases.

In addition, the oil industry organized an astroturf lobbying campaign, a tactic you'll recall we discussed previously.

It's the same one the health care industry used in summer 2009 to make it appear as if ordinary citizens opposed health care reform when, in fact, shills were sent to town hall meetings for the express purpose of disrupting them and confusing the issues.

The Western States Petroleum Association (WSPA), an oil industry trade group, tapped into two consumer groups usually dedicated to the cause of keeping utility bills low: Toward Utility Rate Normalization (TURN) and Utility Consumer's Action Network. Oil companies made a new group called Californians Against Utility Company Abuse (CAUCA) to promote two bills intended to block the government from using utility revenue to build an infrastructure for natural gas and electric vehicles. Calef and Goble wrote:

> CAUCA, managed by the Burlingame-based public relations firm Woodward & McDowell, started its campaign by sending a letter to 200,000 ratepayers urging them to protest against the proposed $600 million utility investments in alternative support systems. The letter, signed by TURN executive director Audrie Krause and by Howard Owens, director of Congress of California Seniors, made no mention that it had been written by Woodward & McDowell or that the whole effort had been paid [for] by the WSPA. About 50,000 citizens returned postcards to Woodward & McDowell, which in turn forwarded the cards to legislators' offices. To further its astroturf strategies, WSPA created fake grassroots movements such as Californians Against Hidden Taxes (CAHT) and the National Institute for Emergency Vehicle Safety, a one-man group that claimed to speak for emergency response workers concerned about hazards related to EVs (such as battery shocks, battery leaks, etc.).

If you want to know how it turned out, look at how many EV1s are on the road in California today: zero. How much gasoline does the oil industry sell in the United States per week? About 3 billion gallons, according to the Environmental Protection Agency.

Lest you think this kind of corporate control happens only in America, take a little detour with me to the United Kingdom, top ally of the United States. Remember how the Iraq war was supposedly all about protecting innocent people from future terrorist attacks? It started as a search for weapons of mass destruction. Then, when there were none, it morphed into a mission to bring democracy to the Iraqi people. It was never about oil, mind you. Pesky protesters kept saying so, even to the point of rudely announcing that Iraq had no connection whatsoever to the 9/11 attacks, but the government insisted the war was never about oil. The United States and its allies, chiefly the United Kingdom, had responded to a higher calling: protecting freedom, keeping citizens from harm, and serving justice to evildoers.

That canard went down in flames in August 2009 when Scotland released a convicted terrorist to his home in Libya in exchange for oil concessions. The speeches about justice and freedom and protection fell mute the moment 44 billion barrels of oil hung in the balance. Arnaud de Borchgrave wrote in the *Washington Times* on August 31, 2009, that "Heated denials notwithstanding, Scotland's 'compassionate release' of convicted Libyan Lockerbie bomber Abdel Baset al-Megrahi was part of a three-way oil deal among Britain, Libya, and Scotland."[16] Sir Mark Allen, former head of the counterterrorism department of Britain's MI6 intelligence service, retired from that post to become a senior executive at the company formerly known as British Petroleum, now known as just BP to obfuscate its line of work. It's the biggest company in Britain and the fifth biggest on Earth. Allen's connections from his counterterrorism days came in handy, but not for countering terrorism. De Borchgrave wrote, "Britain's interest was the same as BP's—a bigger share of Libya's untapped oil reserves, estimated at 44 billion barrels."

Two days after De Borchgrave's article appeared, Stephen Glover wrote in the *Daily Mail*:

> Barely a week ago Lord Mandelson pompously declared that it was "completely implausible" and "offensive" to suggest the Government had connived in the release of the Lockerbie bomber, Abdelbaset Al Megrahi, for commercial reasons. Now leaked letters show that this is precisely what the Government did. It moved heaven and earth to secure the release of Megrahi from a Scottish jail, seemingly to facilitate a multi-billion-pound deal between Libya and BP that might otherwise have been in jeopardy.[17]

You can just picture a politician standing at a lectern, shaking a fist in the air, bellowing, "Our young men and women are fighting for the cause of freedom, catching the terrorists where they live and plot, and sending them back where we can lock them up for life to ensure—" An aide rushes up and whispers something in the politician's ear. The politician nods, and then resumes. "As I was saying, it's unreasonable to keep a convicted terrorist locked up for life. They're people, too. It's time we show compassion by letting this poor man at death's door return to his homeland, where he can die in peace with his family."

That's about how it went. No number of lives lost in the various wars on terrorism could dissuade the government from its mission, but oil could. Libya told BP it would give it a sweet oil deal if Scotland released its convicted Libyan terrorist Megrahi, BP called its bought-off politicians, and Megrahi flew home to a hero's welcome. He stood beside Libyan leader Muammar Gadhafi's son on the stairs of an airplane in Tripoli, where hundreds of supporters cheered as the two men raised their clasped hands in a sign of victory.

Government's main advisors when it comes to military and geopolitical affairs appear to be lobbyists from the defense and oil industries. Big business, again. No new president or prime minister is going to change that. Corporations get what corporations want, because corporations pay. It's hard to accept, but not hard to understand.

Oil dependency is a complicated issue, with more than just oil companies keeping you in expensive gas-burning automobiles. Car companies aren't thrilled about going electric, either, because they lose all the profit they make servicing gas engines, changing motor oil, selling new spark plugs, and such. Also, the EV1 boasted a regenerative braking system that used the car's electronics to help slow down. That reduced wear and tear on the usual mechanical parts of the brakes, which meant fewer parts to replace and repair. Car companies weren't eager to give up that part of their business. This is familiar, as it's the same thinking in much of the medical industry that you read about earlier: it's more profitable to treat sick people than prevent sickness, and it's more profitable to sell cars that need a lot of repair and maintenance than to sell cars that don't. Finally, just going electric doesn't by itself save the environment because the electricity needs to be made somehow, and most of the electricity in the United States is made by burning coal, which is produced by another industry with a strong lobby, which you met in the Jon Stewart "Cap'n Trade" segment on page 78. To get a truly environmentally friendly solution, automobiles would need to go electric and the power grid would need to go nuclear or at least partly alternative.

Nonetheless, with oil dependency as with health care, special interest groups spending the money kept things the way they want them to be, and consumers lost. You're still paying through the nose for expensive, dirty gasoline and maintenance on a car powered by inferior technology; the world still depends on oil from unfriendly nations; and oil companies are still the richest on the planet.

According to The Center for Responsive Politics, the oil and gas industry paid $238 million to campaigns from 1990 to 2008, and in 2008 alone they spent $130 million for the services of 650 lobbyists. They pay to keep people dependent on oil, so people will remain dependent.

Let's look at one more.

Military Spending

> **Party A:** People notice that U.S. military expenditures account for more than 20 percent of government spending and, at more than $650 billion per year, almost match the rest of the world's military expenses combined. They want to cut back on military spending, especially big weapons systems with no enemy in a world of small terrorist threats, and fight fewer wars.

> **Party B:** Defense contractors want to continue making and selling military equipment because it's profitable. The biggest profits come from the biggest weapons systems, so they want to keep those.

A's Spending on Campaigns and Lobbying: $0

B's Spending on Campaigns and Lobbying: $289 million

Do you think military spending will go down? If you said "no," you win! What President Eisenhower described in his 1961 farewell address as "the military industrial complex" has managed to keep spending high, even without the existence of powerful enemies.

In June 2008, Robert Scheer wrote in the *Los Angeles Times*:

> Since the 9/11 attacks, the United States has been on a madcap spending spree on wars and weapons having little, if anything, to do with combating terrorism, nothing to do with the imaginary threat from China and everything to do with sustaining an enormously bloated defense industry threatened with extinction because of the demise of the communist enemy. The fact is, the end of the Cold War was a welcome development for

everyone except for those in the military industrial complex whose profits and jobs, as President Eisenhower famously warned, are rooted in every congressional district.[18]

Few people want to pay for more military spending, but it grows anyway. The first President Bush said in 1992 that communism had died and that "we can stop making the sacrifices we had to make when we had an avowed enemy that was a superpower. Now we can look homeward even more and set right what needs to be set right." Sure. Guess who served as his secretary of defense? Dick Cheney, who would later serve as the second President Bush's vice president, and the strongest advocate of the Iraq war. Again, the more things change, eh?

Following that 1992 call for less military spending, the Pentagon's budget actually did decline in the 1990s as a percentage of gross domestic product. It looked for a moment there that our cynicism was misplaced, but just for a moment. Even two years prior to Bush's comments, in April 1990, the *New York Times* reported, "Military contractors, threatened as never before by shrinking Pentagon budgets, are responding with aggressive lobbying to protect weapons programs worth hundreds of billions of dollars. Companies are turning to new tactics and enlisting help at all levels, from chief executives to minor subcontractors. Alliances are forming between corporations and unions."[19]

They had to work overtime in the 1990s because communism was gone, the United States was the only superpower, and small terrorist outfits could hardly justify huge budgets for nuclear missiles and multibillion-dollar submarines. Or could they? That hung as an open question when, as Scheer wrote, along "came what defense industry lobbyists and their many allies on both sides of the aisle in Congress came to treat as the gift of 9/11, offering dramatic imagery of a new global enemy." Despite the Soviet Cold War threat being one of modern, big weaponry, the United States spent more to fight Al Qaeda and its arsenal of box cutters than it did to stave off the Soviets. Why? By now you know why, but here's Scheer again to confirm: ". . . because politicians from both parties are complicit in the waste of taxpayer dollars on weapons systems that deliver jobs to their home districts and profits to their defense industry campaign contributors. It is a disease of our political system predicted by two of our great wartime generals-turned-president."

They were Washington and Eisenhower, each in his farewell address. President Washington warned America even back then "to guard against the impostures of pretended patriotism." President Eisenhower said that "we must guard against the acquisition of unwarranted influence, whether sought or unsought, by the military industrial complex. The potential for the disastrous rise of misplaced power exists and will persist." Both men were ignored. Scheer concluded, "Sadly, defense spending has become enshrined in our political system as a totem to be worshiped rather than a policy program to be critically examined."

Talk about an industrial victory.

Even Robert Gates, director of central intelligence under the first President Bush and secretary of defense under both the second President Bush and President Obama, pointed out the need for a more reasonable defense budget when he wrote in January 2009, "As much as the U.S. Navy has shrunk since the end of the Cold War, for example, in terms of tonnage, its battle fleet is still larger than the next 13 navies combined—and 11 of those 13 navies are U.S. allies or partners."[20]

One reason exorbitant military spending is possible is that the Federal Reserve makes more money anytime the government wants it. That's the "elastic" money supply you read about earlier, and the banks of the Fed love it. Such borrowed money needs to be repaid by taxpayers, but is just tossed on the debt pile that everybody ignores. It's great for politicians looking to pay back their campaign contributors with fat contracts, great for those military contractors who funded the campaigns, and great for the private banks who lend the money. It's not so great for taxpayers, who lose sons and daughters and wealth in wars that are usually not necessary.

Ron Paul devoted a chapter of his book *End the Fed* to the connection between central bank money printing and war. He wrote:

> It is no coincidence that the century of total war coincided with the century of central banking. When governments had to fund their own wars without a paper money machine to rely upon, they economized on resources. They found diplomatic solutions to prevent war, and after they started a war they ended it as soon as possible.

That last part should strike a chord. Wars have become such a regular part of American life that few people cared when politicians, the Fed, and the military industrial complex somehow spun 19 hijackers flying commercial airliners into buildings on September 11 into wars in Afghanistan and Iraq that have lasted longer than World War II. They've also cost twice as much as World War I and the Korean War, and about one-third more than the Vietnam War. All of those other wars at least involved national enemies with legitimate militaries. The 9/11 incident, on the other hand, involved a band of criminals who weren't even from the countries that the United States attacked in response. Fifteen of the hijackers came from U.S. oil ally Saudi Arabia, two from the United Arab Emirates, one from Egypt, and one from Lebanon. Yet off charged the United States into all-out wars in Afghanistan and Iraq, to spend some $3 trillion in borrowed money, and lose more than 6,000 sons and daughters—so far; the expenses and fatalities grow every month. Nobody questions that a response was needed, but two wars lasting longer than the 100-million-troop global conflict of World War II?

Matthew Hoh joined the Foreign Service early in 2009 after serving as a Marine Corps captain, with combat experience in Iraq. He rose to become in July 2009 the senior U.S. civilian in Afghanistan's Zabul province. In September 2009, he resigned in protest against the war in Afghanistan.

In a four-page letter[21] to the State Department's head of personnel, Hoh wrote that he had "lost understanding of and confidence in the strategic purposes of the United States' presence in Afghanistan," that his resignation was "based not upon how we are pursuing this war, but why and to what end," and that he failed "to see the value or the worth in continued U.S. casualties or expenditures of resources in support of the Afghan government in what is, truly, a 35-year-old civil war."

He rued America's support for the Afghan government with its "glaring corruption and unabashed graft; a president whose confidants and chief advisers comprise drug lords and war crimes villains," and its "election process dominated by fraud and discredited by low voter turnout." Support for such a government reminded him "horribly of our involvement with South Vietnam." His most damning paragraph revealed the war's senselessness:

> I find specious the reasons we ask for bloodshed and sacrifice from our young men and women in Afghanistan. If honest, our stated strategy of securing Afghanistan to prevent al-Qaeda resurgence or regrouping would require us to additionally invade and occupy western Pakistan, Somalia, Sudan, Yemen, etc. . . . More so, the September 11th attacks, as well as the Madrid and London bombings, were primarily planned and organized in Western Europe; a point that highlights the threat is not one tied to traditional geographic or political boundaries. Finally, if our concern is for a failed state crippled by corruption and poverty and under assault from criminal and drug lords, then if we bear our military and financial contributions to Afghanistan, we must

reevaluate and increase our commitment to and involvement in Mexico.

He worried about the cost:

> We are mortgaging our nation's economy on a war, which, even with increased commitment, will remain a draw for years to come. Success and victory, whatever they may be, will be realized not in years, after billions more spent, but in decades and generations. The United States does not enjoy a national treasury for such success and victory.

Hoh concluded with a moving reminder that the real cost of unnecessary war is not just financial:

> Thousands of our men and women have returned home with physical and mental wounds, some that will never heal or will only worsen with time. The dead return only in bodily form to be received by families who must be reassured their dead have sacrificed for a purpose worthy of futures lost, love vanished, and promised dreams unkept. I have lost confidence such assurances can anymore be made. As such, I submit my resignation.

In light of arguments against prolonging the war in Afghanistan, so well presented in Hoh's resignation letter, do you suppose Washington withdrew forces? Do you think President Obama denied the request of General Stanley McChrystal, Commander of U.S. Forces Afghanistan, for additional troops? You already know how it turned out, but anybody familiar with the patterns shown in this book knew during Obama's lengthy deliberations in autumn 2009 how it was going to turn out. When he complained about the war's "mission creep" in September 2009 and said he wanted to narrow it, astute watchers knew he wouldn't. He didn't. When he won the Nobel Peace Prize in October 2009 before having created any peace in the world, perceptive onlookers knew it to be farcical. It was. On December 1, 2009, Obama announced a surge of 30,000 troops, and the war raged on. The following week, he picked up his Nobel Peace Prize in Oslo.

Aside from the war's killing of people, it lands a financially staggering blow to a nation staring into bankruptcy's black hole. The White House said the new troops to Afghanistan would cost about $1 million per soldier or Marine per year, for $30 billion in new spending annually. The Pentagon signaled that the United States had for the first time begun spending more in Afghanistan than Iraq.

Bob Herbert wrote in the *New York Times* one day before Obama's announcement:

> The United States is broken—school systems are deteriorating, the economy is in shambles, homelessness and poverty rates are expanding—yet we're nation-building in Afghanistan, sending economically distressed young people over there by the tens of thousands at an annual cost of a million dollars each. . . . The tougher choice for the president would have been to tell the public that the U.S. is a nation faced with terrible troubles here at home and that it is time to begin winding down a war that veered wildly off track years ago. But that would have taken great political courage. . . . We still haven't learned to recognize real strength, which is why it so often seems that the easier choice for a president is to keep the troops marching off to war.[22]

Wars for no reason cause trouble that justifies more war to quell the trouble. If you were in charge of maximizing profits for the military industrial complex, aren't those the kinds of conflicts you'd hope to see? Maybe that's why they're the kind Washington creates. Syndicated columnist Pat Buchanan wrote in September 2009, "The consequences of a U.S. withdrawal [from Afghanistan] today would be

President Who?

The day after President Obama announced a surge of 30,000 more troops into Afghanistan, filmmaker Michael Moore compared quotes from Obama's speech with quotes from former President Bush. Both sets appear in the table following. The parallels show that it doesn't matter who is president. Government's corporate owners always get what they want, and presidents even re-use the same justifications when giving it to them.

Obama	Bush
"We did not ask for this fight."	"We did not seek this conflict."
"New attacks are being plotted as I speak."	"At this moment . . . terrorists are planning new attacks."
"Our cause is just, our resolve unwavering."	"Our cause is just, our coalition determined."
"This is no idle danger, no hypothetical threat."	"The enemies of freedom are not idle."
"We have no interest in occupying your country."	"I wouldn't be happy if I were occupied, either."

far greater than if we had never gone in, or had gone in, knocked over the Taliban, run al-Qaida out of the country, gotten out and gone home." Not going in at all was out of the question, and a quick in-and-out operation would have been too efficient. Instead, American leaders decided to try building an Afghan democracy. Since Afghanistan doesn't want it, making democracy the goal is a perfect path to endless war. It doesn't make sense militarily, but sure is good for business.

Here's Ron Paul again, from his book, *End the Fed*:

Since World War II, the U.S. government has expanded its reach with a shocking voraciousness both at home and abroad. It's been one war after another, the building of killer weapons of mass destruction, the construction of a huge welfare state that covers all classes in society. There was the Cold War, the Korean War, the Bay of Pigs, an invasion of the Dominican Republic, Vietnam, and endless involvement in the Middle East in addition to wars on Nicaragua, Salvador, Bosnia, and Haiti, as well as the wars around the world conducted in the name of the War on Terror. And after every major crisis, whether 9/11, the dot-com disaster of 1999, or the economic meltdown of 2008, the response is more monetary expansion.

Military spending is responsible for a huge portion of America's national debt. Remember the $700 billion in TARP funds taken from the Treasury and given to banks by former Goldmanoid Hank Paulson? You may feel outraged at that, as well you should, but the United States spends almost that much money *every year* on the military.

Massachusetts Democratic Congressman Barney Frank wrote in *The Nation*[23] in February 2009 that the TARP was "a smaller drain on taxpayer dollars than the Iraq war will have cost us by the time it is concluded, and it is roughly equivalent to the $651 billion we will spend on all defense in this fiscal year." He wanted to cut defense spending. "If, beginning one year from now, we were to cut military spending by 25 percent from its projected levels, we would still be immeasurably stronger than any combination of nations with whom we might be engaged. . . . The math is compelling: if we do not make reductions approximating 25 percent of the military budget starting fairly soon, it will be impossible to continue to fund an adequate level of domestic activity even with a repeal of Bush's tax cuts for the very wealthy."

Ten months later, Obama *increased* military spending with his surge of troops to Afghanistan. On top of the eight years the United States had already fought there, how many more years did Obama add, and for what?

You know by now the odds of military spending coming down, based simply on the amount of money spent by the defense industry on campaign contributions and lobbying. According to The Center for Responsive Politics, the defense sector paid $139 million to campaigns from 1990 to 2008, and in 2008 alone they spent $150 million for the services of 1,000 lobbyists.

They pay to keep military spending high, so that's where it will stay.

What They Have in Common

With a focus on money and how decisions get made, we looked at three social issues: health care, oil dependency, and military spending. What do they have in common? All three are managed in a way that is good for corporate interests and bad for citizens. In each industry, financial people everywhere at the top fight to keep in place a racket that swindles people below.

Pick Your Puppet

The raw honesty of comedians helps them cut through layers of lies and PR spin to shout out what's really going on. Earlier, you read Jon Stewart's "Cap'n Trade" segment, George Carlin's pitch-perfect summary of American society, and Stephen Colbert's idea for avoiding preexisting conditions in the health insurance industry. Now, look at a few things the late Bill Hicks said about corporate control of Washington politics. The following lightly edited excerpts are from his 1997 album *Rant in E-Minor*:

> They're all the same. I'll show you politics in America. Here it is, right here.

"I think the puppet on the right shares my beliefs."

"I think the puppet on the left is more to my liking."

"Hey, wait a minute, there's one guy holding up both puppets!"

"Shut up! Go back to bed, America, your government is in control. Here's Love Connection, watch this and get fat and stupid. By the way, keep drinking beer, you morons.". . .

I knew Billy Clinton became one of the boys when he bombed Iraq. Remember that? It was just a little news story for two days, isn't that interesting? He launched 22 cruise missiles against Baghdad in retaliation for the alleged assassination attempt against George Bush, which failed. We killed six innocent people launching 22, I think three-million-dollars-apiece missiles, on Baghdad. I think that's a little bit overdoing it, if you ask me. . . .

I have this feeling, because you know there's the handful of people actually run everything. That's true, it's provable, I'm not a conspiracy nut, it's provable. Handful, a very small elite run and own these corporations, which include the mainstream media. I have this feeling who's ever elected president, like Clinton was, no matter what promises you promise on the campaign trail, blah blah blah, when you win you go into this smoky room with the 12 industrialist, capitalist scumbags who got you in there, and you're in this smoky room and this little film screen comes down. And a big guy with a cigar (says), "Roll the film." And it's a shot of the Kennedy assassination from an angle you've never seen before, that looks suspiciously off the grassy knoll, and then the film screen goes up and the lights come up and they go to the new president, "Any questions?"

"Uh, just what my agenda is."

"First, we bomb Baghdad."

"You got it."

In the case of health care, corporations want government out of the sector because it keeps a national system impossible. A national health care system would be cheaper for citizens, and provide more of them with coverage. Ideally, it would provide *all* of them with coverage. The private health care system is profitable for corporations, but costs citizens much more and leaves millions of them without coverage. Because the corporations pay to keep government out of health care, government is mostly out and the private system persists.

In the case of oil dependency, corporations want to keep selling oil until it's gone. They pay for government support and they get it. Government mandates for alternative energy and tax incentives to encourage its widespread adoption are missing in action. Even political candidates who get into office on promises of ending our dependence on oil, never make progress. Look at Obama. He said in his presidential campaign that he would reduce dependence on foreign oil and maintain a ban on offshore drilling, specifically mentioning Florida repeatedly. Then, just seven months after entering the White House, he lent $2 billion of U.S. taxpayer money to Brazil's state-owned oil company, Petrobras, so it could explore offshore drilling near Rio de Janeiro. That increased U.S. dependence on foreign oil and supported offshore drilling. He might quibble by saying Petrobras will drill off non-American shores but, come on, it's the same Atlantic Ocean lapping Florida and Rio.

In the case of military spending, corporations want government to buy expensive weapons systems. Little attention is paid to whether enemies exist or, even if they do, what kinds of enemies. That's why we have enough nuclear missiles on nuclear submarines to wipe any nation off the map, but couldn't protect the World Trade Center. We're armed for world war, but not for a world filled with little wars. Too bad we live in the latter.

Corporate interests cry out in protest against any government spending on health care, calling it irresponsible and pointing to the runaway national debt. Yet, corporate interests say nothing of debt when it comes to military spending, even though it eats up almost one-third of tax revenue when expanded to include supplementary spending for the Iraq and Afghanistan wars, the Department of Veteran's Affairs, and the Department of Homeland Security, according to the fiscal 2008 financial statement of the Government Accountability Office. Support for government spending has nothing to do with the issues. It has everything to do with how such spending will affect corporate profits. In health care, government spending hurts corporations, so it's opposed. In the military, government spending helps corporations, so it's supported.

Remember all the debate about whether the United States could afford national health care? Notice, you never hear it asked whether the United States can afford another war. That's just assumed, a necessary expense, gotta do what we gotta do. It's the same Treasury paying, though. The money wasted on the Iraq war alone could have covered an American health care program. The Treasury that can't afford health care has no trouble affording war. Absolute accounting doesn't exist in Washington, only special interest accounting does. Whatever numbers work for corporations are the ones that make their way to the top.

Government doesn't care about you. It cares about corporations.

Think Like a Corporation

Admit it, you thought this chapter was getting off the book's subject. You thought we'd jumped the shark, talking about politics, lobbyists, health care, oil, and the military. You thought maybe I was trying to foist political opinions on you, in a book about guarding your financial freedom.

In fact, we never strayed off subject. We couldn't have been more on subject as to why your personal finances are in danger everywhere you turn. Beyond the great taxpayer stick-up that transferred gazillions from the Treasury to big banks, nearly every other aspect of society is aligned to take your wealth. What is presented to you as a social issue is always about money. There's no need to argue points, just look at the financial breakdown. Those who pay the most get what they want. The reason there's a constant debate about health care in America is that the profitable industry doesn't want it to become a public service with no profit motive. That's not about health; it's about money. The only reason you have no choice when it comes to the type of energy that powers your car is that oil is the most profitable business on Earth. It's not about the environment, technology, or convenience, the things that are usually discussed on the subject; it's about money. When it comes to the military, America hasn't fought a worthwhile war in six decades. Freedom and defense and other patriotic prosaisms are really about profit for defense contractors. That's why there's always an enemy, a war without end, a necessary military action. It's not about protecting anything; it's about money.

Financial people infest the top ranks of every part of society, jacking up the ramps of commerce at an angle straight into their bank accounts. Financially stupid people infest the populace, supporting causes that cost them money and opposing others that would save them money.

While the most recent focus was on the economic disaster that came from too many people borrowing more than they could afford to repay, it's not the only strand on society's spider web through which your money needs to pass. Each sticky strand tries to snag your dollars. The thickest, stickiest one is taxes for government so politicians can redirect your money to their banking and big business supporters. What do you get out of it? Banks offering schemes that are bad for your finances, expensive private health insurance, expensive oil-powered cars, and wars for nothing. What a deal!

We all have opinions on the underlying social issues behind each subject, but those opinions are irrelevant to this discussion on finances. The only relevant part is that each subject comes down to money. That money is supplied by you. Ultimately, you're the one paying exorbitant health care costs and insurance premiums, you're the one pumping expensive gasoline into your car and paying expensive maintenance on the internal combustion engine, you're the one funding every military program through tax revenue. Pundits can make all the clever, well-reasoned points they want, but decisions are made by dollars, not discussions. While passionate debates rage, the money keeps flowing to precisely the groups who pay to receive it. It's true what you've heard: it's all about the money. Let your guard down and the array of pickpockets will bankrupt you faster than a politician can shake hands at a fundraising event.

One of the best ways to see through the fog of corporate-sponsored disinformation and lobbying on these and other social issues is to think like a corporation yourself. Tune out every angle except the money, and see what viewpoint best supports your financial interest. Doing so reveals a crystal-clear path to reclaiming the economic landscape. Let's see how two voters acting in their own best financial interests, just as corporations do, would handle the three issues we discussed. I'll name the two voters Frank and Frieda Fiscal.

On health care, Frank and Frieda realize that they pay a lot in taxes but still have to find their own private health insurance and pay high-priced premiums. If a system like Medicare were available to them using the taxes they already pay, they'd save a lot of money. So, they're in favor of a national health insurance plan run on the tax revenue government already collects, because it would save them money. It also doesn't hurt that they'd avoid fighting a corporate bureaucracy every time they need care.

On oil dependency, Frank and Frieda see that they're getting fleeced every month for automobile maintenance and gasoline. If government would mandate lower or zero emission standards and bolster them with tax incentives for making and using electric cars, for instance, there would be a quick abundance of alternatives to gasoline-powered models. An electric car would save Frank and Frieda bundles of money by reducing maintenance and eliminating gasoline. So, they're in favor of government measures to encourage smarter vehicles. It also doesn't hurt that they'd avoid the inconvenience of stopping at gas stations, and they like the environmental benefit offered by zero-emission vehicles.

On military spending, Frank and Frieda realize that not one war in their adult lifetimes has done anything for the country or their own bottom lines. No other nation attacked the United States. When the United States was attacked by terrorists, the proper response did not require full-scale wars in unrelated places. Reducing the oversized military budget and restricting wars to only those that defend the nation would free up enough of Frank and Frieda's tax money to pay for their national health insurance, and maybe help in other ways, such as reducing the cost of sending their kids to college. So, they're in favor of reducing the military budget.

Seen through the lens of personal financial benefit, issues of the day clear up in a hurry. It requires a grasp of the whole landscape, though, which is why special interests compartmentalize and focus like a laser on one point that makes sense in isolation but not in context. For example, one of the complaints voiced against national health insurance was that it might raise taxes for some high-income earners. First, that wouldn't be necessary if government stopped giving away trillions of taxpayer dollars to banking cronies and spending $650 billion per year on the military. Second, even higher taxes might be worth it if the need to buy expensive private health insurance disappeared and the overall cost of health care dropped, which it would do under the watchful eye of a single payer like Medicare.

Focusing on finances helps cut through double standards. For instance, why is socialism terrible when it provides health care for citizens, but wonderful when it bails out bad banks and builds bombs? Health care for all? No, because that's socialism. Bank bailouts and bombs? Yes, because those are public-private partnerships. Government giveaways are called socialism only when they *don't* benefit corporations. If they do benefit corporations, they're called systemically important, or patriotic, or the American way. The following list compares corporate interests with citizen interests across a variety of social issues:

Corporate Interest	Citizen Interest
Keep health care profitable.	Make health care affordable.
Keep selling oil until it's gone.	Stop using oil as soon as possible.
Fight wars to keep military spending up.	Stop fighting wars, for many reasons.
Receive bailout money from the Treasury.	Let failed companies fail.
Inflate the money supply to reduce the value of savings, raise prices, and encourage borrowing and spending.	Enjoy a stable money supply so savings retain value over time, prices don't rise, and debt is less tempting.

Notice that society has gone the corporate way in each case, while citizens are hung out to dry. Health care is expensive, oil dependency persists, worthless wars continue, military spending is rising, the government continues bailing out failed corporations, and the Federal Reserve is inflating the money supply. Score 6 for corporations, 0 for citizens.

In this book, we're not trying to fix the corruption of our society, we're trying to understand its causes. Instead of looking for ways to change things, we're looking at why things never change. The system is bought off, wrapped up, locked down, covered over, and thoroughly denied. Anybody born into the bottom 95 percent of the population faces a machine built by a century of intermingling among society's racketeers. Make sure you understand that, so you see why it's necessary to guard your wealth against the plunderers angling for it. Assume they will attack, and prepare your defenses.

Knowing what you now know of government, banks, and big business, don't you find it disgraceful that so many rubes trusted banks to lend them money at good terms, and thought government would protect them? That's like hogs trusting butchers to give them feed without consequence, and thinking the grocery store will protect them. Alas, there's a never-ending supply of rubes and hogs on this planet, and the banks and governments and butchers and grocery stores have gotten pretty darned good at driving them in the right direction.

Corporate Socialism

In the Federal Reserve section of Chapter 4, you encounter a woman named Elizabeth Warren. She's the Harvard professor and chair of the Congressional Oversight Panel for the Troubled Asset Relief Program who told the *Washington Post* why inflation has made it harder for the middle class to get ahead. On November 5, 2009, she discussed government guarantees with James Surowiecki at the *New Yorker*. Knowing more about the TARP's $700-billion bailout of banks than almost anybody, she brings a valuable perspective. She told Surowiecki:

> The old rules of regulation just literally don't work anymore. Because now we're under this giant shadow of explicit and implicit government guarantees. . . . We crossed a threshold last September and October when we said, in effect, with major financial institutions in the United States, we will pump money in and your shareholders will still hold the shares, your management team will still run the show, and your debt holders—including your general, unsecured debt— will get 100 cents on the dollar; in other words, we will throw as many taxpayers as we need to throw under the bus to keep your business functionally operational in the way that it was operational before, without cost to you personally and to your shareholders personally. That's a whole new world.

> You bet it's a whole new world, called corporate social-ism. Corporations keep all the profit, taxpayers shoulder all the risk. If Uncle Sam backstopped any venture you dreamed up, wouldn't you dream big and manage recklessly? Sure, because you'd have nothing to lose. That's called moral haz-ard, and the government varnished the nation with it in the subprime mortgage bailout bonanza. Heads, corporations win; tails, taxpayers lose.
>
> *Source:* Elizabeth Warren, Interview with James Surowiecki, *New Yorker,* November 5, 2009), www.newyorker.com/online/blogs/jamessurowiecki/2009/11/video-elizabeth-warren.html.

Stop Trusting and Start Going It Alone

If you're waiting for society to wake up, you'd best get com-fortable. You need to stop dreaming about a world of hon-est bankers, fair business leaders, and fault-free politicians. More importantly, you need to stop trusting them with your financial future. Anybody trusting that collection of back-slapping opportunists is a sucker.

In these pages, you and I are not concerned with whether Republicans or Democrats are better, or with our own opin-ions on issues like health care, oil, and military spending. We're not really even looking at whether politicians are good or bad people. We can grant that presidents try to improve life for Americans. Let's say they set out with the best of inten-tions and work as hard as they can in the best ways they know how. Fine, but nothing changes. Before new presidents know which number to dial for the White House kitchen, their glo-rious campaign vision is hog-tied by special interest groups who know their way around Washington better than any poli-tician. Want to know a great place to eat or get free tickets to a concert in Washington? Ask a lobbyist, not a leader.

The salient point for us is that the political system was built for and is run by people whose interests are not necessarily aligned with ours. You can be sure that Washington gives a lot more thought to what Goldman Sachs needs than it does to what you need. Bet your life that lobbyists know the names of the sons and daughters of corporate executives, but don't know a thing about you. When push comes to shove, and it always does, whose interests are going to come out on top, the corporation's or yours? Take a guess, and follow the money for a hint. How much did you contribute to the Obama campaign? Just for argument's sake, let's say zero. Now, how much do you think Goldman Sachs, Citigroup, JPMorgan Chase, and Morgan Stanley contributed? According to the Center for Responsive Politics, those four financial giants together gave the Obama campaign $2.9 million. They didn't do it directly, of course, what with all the pesky contribution limits put in place to make people think nobody's bought off, but their bundled contributions from individual members and political organizations came to that much. Obama's total take from the financial sector, when expanded to include accounting, banking, insurance, investment, real estate, and securities, came to $34.8 million. Interestingly, his opponent, John McCain, collected $28.6 million from the same groups. See why the real people in charge don't care who becomes president? Just as Altria's Philip Morris tobacco division couldn't care less whether you get your nicotine through Marlboro or Virginia Slims cigarettes because it owns both brands, so corporate interests couldn't care less whether voters elect this politician or that one because they own both.

Nonetheless, starry-eyed voters fell for the change gambit again, looked to Obama to do the right thing in the financial crisis, and expressed shock when what he did was the same thing Bush had done: gave taxpayer money to big banks. What voters didn't realize is that it never mattered who won the election.

Immediately after winning, Obama appointed Illinois Democratic Congressman Rahm Emanuel as White House chief of staff. The *Wall Street Journal* reported in November 2008 that Emanuel "earned $16.2 million in a two-year stint working in Chicago for investment-banking firm Wasserstein Perella & Co." In his last House race in 2008, he "collected more money than any other House member from hedge funds, private-equity firms, and the broader securities and investment industry, even though he faced no serious opposition." The *Journal* found that since Emanuel was elected to Congress six years prior, he had "raised $1.5 million in campaign donations from Wall Street employees, making the industry the single largest backer of his political career, according to the nonpartisan Center for Responsive Politics."[24] Follow Emanuel's path through Congress and you'll see why. He sat on the House Financial Services Committee and later on the Ways and Means Committee, both connected to Wall Street. The banksters owned the man just elected president, and within days that man chose as his highest ranking staff member another owned asset of the financial club. It never ends.

Charles Krauthammer asked in the *Washington Post* in September 2009, "What happened to President Obama? His wax wings having melted, he is the man who fell to earth. What happened to bring his popularity down further than that of any new president in polling history save Gerald Ford (post-Nixon pardon)?" Krauthammer looked back on the way Obama had come into office fancying himself a "tribune of the people, spokesman for the grass roots, harbinger of a new kind of politics from below that would upset the established lobbyist special-interest order of Washington." Instead, like all the others, Obama ended up "cutting backroom deals with every manner of special interest—from drug companies to auto unions to doctors—in which favors worth billions were quietly and opaquely exchanged."[25]

Society won't change. Politicians will always be owned by special interests, and voters will always fall for the same broken promises—even when the politicians themselves complain that it's always been this way as they head off to Washington to keep it this way even longer, the way Obama did. Other people might never catch on, but you should.

It's time to stop trusting and start going it alone.

Forget the debt dopes behind this latest mess, the ones who fell for every line from government and big business. Forget the army of idiots with their credit cards, the purveyors of trifles, the enticing advertisements, the buy-now-pay-later gimmicks, the new-boss-same-as-the-old-boss political system, the lobbyists running government, the big bank bailouts, the alphabet soup of toxic idiocy, the corporate astroturf campaigns, the never-ending wars, the painfully profitable oil addiction, the voluntary indentured servitude, and the country's chain debt habit.

They have corrupted the promise of America.

This fraudulent backdrop has turned citizens into cash generation units, nothing more. Everywhere you turn, there's a claim on your wealth. Sometimes it's government cranking up the taxes so it has more revenue to redirect to its corporate sponsors, sometimes it's banks influencing government to get the regulations they need to be able to trick more consumers into bad deals, sometimes it's corporations filling society with wasteful ways to give up money. When it all comes together at the Ranch of Financial Calamity, most consumers get roped in, tied to the cart, and whipped into a life of walking the circular path. When they don't actively resist, they end up bankrupt at the feet of a society that was always out to get them.

The current U.S. passport is filled with scenes from our nation's proud history, the image we have of ourselves and our great land. How does bankruptcy fit into that? You don't see on passport pages any pictures of credit cards, or stacks of bills, or no-doc home loans, or shady financial firms. Those are too shameful to show up in our national self-image, so why aren't they too shameful for our national lifestyle? They should be. The modern economy turned our land of the free and home of the brave into the land of the fee and home of the slave.

Look into the eagle's eye on a passport signature page and decide what kind of American you want to be. A bankrupt victim crying for help from the same bastards who cleaned you out? A debt dope with no self control? Of course not. Earn the right to carry that passport and call yourself American by getting your financial house in order and standing sublime against the fraudulent backdrop. Become a living reminder to those around you that rugged individualism put America on the map and is needed now to keep America on the map. Maybe a few miserable debtors will see your financial gallantry and get up off their knees to join you.

Don't wait for government to make you that gallant citizen. It's not the country that makes the people, but the people that make the country. Rodney Rube's bad financial decisions matter to the nation, and it's high time he starts making better ones. Same with his neighbors, and their relatives, and mine, and yours. When a rube buys a house he can't afford and then loses it, values of all homes in the neighborhood are negatively affected. When enough rubes do it together, the whole economy blows up. We need to fix ourselves individually in order to fix the nation collectively. Politicians won't do it, because the system works for them. Bankers won't do it, because the system works for them. Businesses won't do it, because the system works for them. We have to do it, because the system doesn't work for us.

There's nothing you can do to change the behavior of others. You can change only your behavior and guarantee yourself alone a life of financial freedom that makes the nation stronger.

Let's think more about that.

7

Financial Freedom

Most people talk about financial freedom as if it's a far-off goal, something that only those on the Forbes 400 list of richest Americans have experienced. It's not. Financial freedom has nothing to do with net worth. It has everything to do with money management, no matter what amount of money we're talking about.

Understanding how little of your money is actually yours is important for knowing why you have to manage it well. To that end, we'll look at your low-battery birth to see that only one third of your income is unclaimed by special interests. Once you get that, we'll explore how financial freedom comes from the way you manage your one third, not from how much it's worth.

Your Low-Battery Birth

Society is so thoroughly constructed around draining your wealth that at the moment of your birth, you operated on a low financial battery. Only about one third of your lifetime income is controlled by you. Special interests already claimed the other two thirds before you were born. With such a small margin of error, if you make even a few of the common financial mistakes, you're doomed. There's too little money left to help you recover.

The battery in Figure 7.1 represents your lifetime income. Each section of the battery is one third of your income. Government, banks, and big business spent decades carefully plugging into your lifetime income battery before you had a name. You didn't even know what money was, but already somewhere around two thirds of what you'd earn over your lifetime was claimed by the system on the day you drew your first breath. No wonder it's a challenge to break free.

The top section of the battery is the money you lose to taxes. We all have to pay them, but we receive little worthwhile in return for the money we sacrifice. In the United States, so much tax revenue is gobbled up by corporate special interests that there isn't enough left to provide citizens with services they need. Instead, tax dollars flow to bad banks whose Washington cronies orchestrate bailouts, to

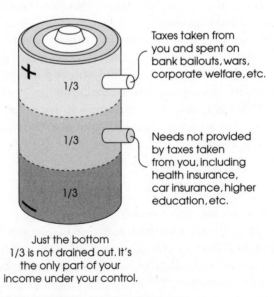

Figure 7.1   Your Lifetime Income Battery

subsidies that prop up inefficient corporations, to defense contractors for wars that benefit only them, and so on.

The middle section of the battery is the money you have to spend on all the needs that aren't provided by your taxes. You don't get health insurance from government, so you have to pay for it yourself. Government doesn't enforce reasonable pricing within the health care industry, so you have to pay exorbitant prices yourself. Your car registration doesn't include car insurance, so you're legally required to buy it yourself. Government doesn't provide you or your children with a college education, so you have to pay for it yourself.

The bottom section of the battery is the money you have left after paying taxes and buying the services your taxes don't provide. That's all you have to work with. The other two thirds are gone—zap!—into government, bank, and big business money chests. Given the extreme disadvantage you face, it's easy to see why you need to manage that one third of your income very carefully if you're ever going to get ahead. If you blow that one third, too, you have nothing left. Many Americans find themselves in just that situation.

People who object to government being involved in anything are fine by me as long as they also insist on government therefore collecting less tax money from us. Release most of the money tied up in wasted taxes and the battery's picture changes, doesn't it? Suddenly, that top third of the battery lost to taxes would shrink, leaving a lot more money for us to buy the services we need on our own and still have more left for ourselves. Personally, that's what I'd like to see, with a truly free market determining which companies live and die based on how well they serve their customers. The best option is low taxes that enable people to use the money saved to provide for their own needs in a free market. That appears impossible, so the next best option is higher taxes that at least provide needed services. Instead, American society has morphed into the worst combination: high taxes with few benefits.

By now, you know why. Companies encourage government spending on things that profit corporations, such as bailouts and bombs. Companies discourage government spending on things that benefit citizens, such as health care.

Keep the low-battery birth image prominent in your mind. See it every time you consider a major purchase or other financial decision. Be sure you make the right moves to get the most out of the one third of your income that's yours. Don't let even the small amount of money under your control end up drained out the same two wires that already drain away most of your wealth.

Rich Gone Wrong

Richard Grant was kind enough to share his story with me because he thought it would help people better manage their money. He's a general contractor and his wife is a chiropractor. They lived in South Lake Tahoe, California, in the early 2000s, and their combined net income was $250k per year.

Richard parlayed that into more wealth in the real estate market. In 2000, he bought a building lot for $16k, added permits and plans for another $22k, and sold the package for $119k in just three months. Encouraged by that, he bought a duplex the following year for $150k and sold it two years later for $295k. The buoyant housing market looked like the fast track to the good life, as it did to many Americans at that time, and Richard used the proceeds from selling the duplex to put 20 percent down on a bigger home that cost $515k, partly because he wanted more space to care for his mother-in-law. He and his wife watched with glee as the new home's value shot to $1.2 million over the next few years.

The Grants used that paper value as collateral to buy a paint shop for him, a chiropractic office for her, and raw land for them to eventually build their retirement home. The mortgage payments on all the real estate came to $7,500 per month. When times were good, that was no problem. The Grants enjoyed resplendent restaurants and a home so chockablock with niceties that items still in boxes with price tags spilled from open doors.

They didn't notice that it all came from the rising real estate market, to which they'd hitched their whole wagon. Should that market hit a bump or, just maybe, crash like an Indy 500 racer into the wall at 150 mph in an explosion of sparks and sprockets, the ride in the Grant wagon could become a touch unsettling. The U.S. housing market became that racer, revved past 150 mph, and hit the wall.

Richard's wife grew ill, to the point that she needed to close her practice. The loss of her income coupled with her growing medical expenses strained the family's reserves. When the economy turned south, Richard's jobs shrank in size and number, then disappeared entirely when the local tourism business slowed in the bigger economic contraction. The value of the Grant real estate portfolio collapsed, putting it underwater by hundreds of thousands of dollars. The Grants tried short selling but found no buyers, and their properties entered foreclosure. In summer 2009, they packed up, mailed the house keys to the bank, and moved in with their son's family in Denver.

Even that wasn't the end of it. On top of the properties they lost, they also gave up some $200k in down payments and equity. They owe money on their vehicles, credit cards, and education via unpaid student loans. At a time when they thought they'd be planning retirement, they're instead planning bankruptcy.

Richard says his biggest mistake was taking on so much debt that servicing it required two incomes. Had one income been sufficient, he and his wife would have been able to handle the closing of her practice, her rising medical bills, and the evaporating paper value of their real estate. They would have been better prepared for the loss of his income, as well, because their savings would have been bigger.

Richard's son in Denver, Darin Grant, who contributes his story further on in this book to show how his careful money management enabled him to help his father and step-mother through the recession, told me that he came home one night in October 2009 to find his father resting in bed. Richard told Darin that he'd been climbing up and down ladders for six hours that day, and was beat. "I never thought I'd still be doing this at this stage of my life," he said.

I hope Richard and his wife find a path to recovery, both medically and financially, and I think they will. He told me just after Thanksgiving 2009 that "thanks to Darin's gener-osity in providing us an oasis in these trying times, my wife will be getting a new hip on the 21st of December, and that should be the end of the medical gauntlet." I admire the Grants's desire to help others avoid their financial fate. Their story shows that how we manage our money matters more than the amount we have to manage.

More Money, Same Story

There's always a bigger fish, and it can always beach itself. The *San Luis Obispo Tribune* reported in November 2009 that David Weyrich, whom it described as "one of the most promi-nent businessmen in the county," faced foreclosure on several of his prize properties, "including the Paso Robles winery bear-ing his name and the luxury inn Villa Toscana."

Weyrich reportedly cleared $200 million in 1998 when he sold a billboard business begun by his father-in-law. He invested the proceeds in real estate, newspapers, a business-jet leasing com-pany, vineyards and wineries, and a yacht. By the end of 2009, he had fallen behind in payments or debt service to more than 150 vendors, lenders, and other parties. Despite his immense wealth, Weyrich overextended himself and became cash poor.

Source: Melanie Cleveland, "David Weyrich Facing Foreclosure on Villa Toscana, York Mountain and Martin and Weyrich Wineries and His Home," *San Luis Obispo Tribune*, November 13, 2009, www.sanluisobispo .com/178/story/920170.html.

Nobody is exempt from the laws of money management, and no amount of money is too large to squander. Whatever amount is yours, manage it well so that you can live well.

What You Do with Your Money

Your lifestyle depends more on what you do with your money than on how much you make. Financial freedom is not for the rich alone. Anybody can live financially free.

A woman making $20,000 per month is not financially free if she spends $25,000 per month. A woman making $4,000 per month is financially free if she spends less than $3,200 per month—less than 80 percent of her take-home pay. Financial freedom is the feeling you get when you abide by the First Rule of Finance. Living within your means frees you from jobs you don't like and places you don't want to live. It presents a path to wherever you want to go, because you know how to decide what you want and put away the money needed to get it. That something might be living abroad for a while. It might be opening your own business. It might be going back to school. It might be a house on a hill. It might be a ranch in the mountains. Whatever it is for you, smart money management will make it possible.

Life lived on a pile of cash is better than life lived under a pile of debt. Imagine how different Monday morning looks to Rich Robert, who has $100,000 in the bank, than it looks to Poor Paul, who has $100,000 on 13 credit cards at 18 percent. Just about whatever Rich Robert sees, he can buy. Just about whatever Poor Paul saw, he did buy or, rather, financed. Now that he's awash in all those depreciating trifles, Poor Paul is bored with them but feels constricted, a snake around his neck, because the payments are killing him—but there's so much more he wants! He needs, needs, needs, but can no longer get, get, get. Rich Robert doesn't need. He got that emotion under control years ago and now that he can buy anything he sees in the store or at the dealership, he's in no hurry to get any of it. He enjoys thinking about what he wants, leisurely, with the comfort of knowing he can get it whenever he decides.

You know what it comes down to? Nobody has a hold on Rich Robert. They can't tie him down to a job he hates. They can't jerk him around with changing interest rates. They can't tell him he doesn't have enough vacation days to take his wife to Montego Bay. He's a free man, and all because he spent a few years saving a few bucks of take-home pay.

That adds up more quickly than most people think. According to CareerBuilder.com, the average starting salary in 2008 for a graduate with a liberal arts degree was $33,000; with an accounting degree $47,000; and with an engineering degree $56,000. For single filers with no federal allowances and a state income tax rate of 5 percent, those respective annual salaries turned into monthly after tax take-home pay of $2,070 for liberal artists, $2,860 for accountants, and $3,350 for engineers. Each abiding by the First Rule of Finance would save per month a respective $400, $600, and $700, after rounding to the nearest $100. Let's say they started working right out of college at age 22. Even assuming no salary increases, bonuses, or other income boosting events, these three types of people would see bank balances of $38k, $58k and $67k when they turn 30. Because anybody smart enough to do that is also smart enough to grow their income and learn a few things about investing, I'm confident the balances would actually be much higher.

Which brings us back to Rich Robert. Don't assume he grew up sucking a silver spoon. He's not necessarily from a rich family. He might just be an English major who figured out how to save a few bucks, an accountant who restrained himself, an engineer who understood how to divide by five. (Did I lose you? Take-home pay divided by five gives you the 20 percent you should be saving.) Robert is rich not in the way a billionaire is rich. He's rich because he achieved financial freedom on *his* income. He lived within *his* means. He made *his* own life. Along with the money his financial management brought him, it also brought him pride and confidence, I dare say, even manhood.

It may please you to know that of those three starting salary categories, I landed firmly in the lowest out of college. I studied English literature at the University of Colorado, and I paid my own way. I was surrounded by rich kids from California carrying credit cards from their parents. The bills went straight to California so the kids never even saw them. They went skiing on weekends; I went to my part-time job delivering sandwiches. They made fun of my beat-up old car; I was just glad to keep it running on meager wages.

When I was a senior, I applied to work at IBM. The company invited me to its Silicon Valley Laboratory in San Jose, California. I told the human resources manager that I didn't think I could afford to get there, and asked if I could interview instead at the local Boulder plant. There was a pause, then he said that IBM would pay for my transportation. I thanked him profusely, bought the best suit I could afford, and flew to the Silicon Valley Laboratory for a test and series of interviews, and IBM offered me a job as a technical writer. I was elated. I keep a special smile for Big Blue because of that break. It was the only company that believed in me. I never knew the meaning of the term "competing offer."

When I graduated, I did so with student loan debt and it drove me crazy. I barely made the trip to California in that beat-up car of mine, found the cheapest apartment near the lab, and lived the life of a pauper until those student loans were paid in full. I scrounged my way to a zero balance within a year, driving that same old car the whole time. I parked it on the far edge of the IBM lot, in the shadows of trees.

Once I got to zero, I kept the Spartan lifestyle going and saved a nest egg for investing. It hit $1,000, then $5,000, then $20,000, and in less than four years of aggressive saving and some good investments, it topped $100,000. I rewarded myself with a—no, not a new car—a *newer* used car.

With respect and gratitude, I bid adieu to IBM because I knew within two weeks of my arrival that corporate life was not for me when a senior writer said, "If you want to know where you'll be in ten years, just look at someone who's been here ten years longer than you." I did so, and promised myself I'd never make it past five.

IBM was the only "real" job I've ever had. I started my own company after leaving. In running one's own company, financial management becomes even more important. My company has never spent one day in debt. All new ventures are financed with positive cash flow. All mistakes I pay for myself. Most profits I use to grow the business. It's not a bank that makes it possible. It's not credit cards (even though one came in handy during that book printing episode I mentioned earlier). It's smart financial management.

Your own financial freedom can begin right now. It's not far off in the future, it's today. It's not what you make, it's what you keep. It's not a bank balance, it's a determination. Pride springs not from having things, but from accomplishing things. The actions you take to be able to afford the objects of your dreams are infinitely more important than the objects.

Every rich person I know would be more impressed with the story of how you were able to pay cash for that lovely car than with the car itself. If you drive up in a new luxury car and I ask how you paid for it and you say, "I just borrowed a bunch of money from a bank," do you think I'll be impressed? Not at all. That's nothing special. Any idiot with a pen can do that. Now, tell me how you worked your business hard for five years, putting away all your savings each month while looking at a picture of the car pinned to your office wall, then paid cash one glorious day . . . now *that's* a story! I'd shake your hand. I'd thank the stars that my country counts you among its citizenry.

Things are just things. Accomplishments are character.

I learned this from a rich man in my family, my uncle who lives in Newport Beach, California. He's the most financially successful of his siblings, and is often called upon to help those "in over their heads" from his own immediate family and a long list of relatives. Probably every third phone call to his house ends up costing him money. He never said so, but I know from talking to other people with money that constant requests for financial help get old. "Can't anybody figure it out?" they wonder.

One year, I took my uncle and aunt to a fancy seaside restaurant where *I paid*. I was young and not rich, certainly nowhere near as well-off as they, but I was on my way up and had enough money for the lunch and wanted to show that to my uncle and aunt. You should have seen him beam when I reached for the bill and said it was on me. At first, he seemed unsure what to do. The urge to insist it was his treat may have flickered in his mind, but dissipated when he saw my determination. He probably couldn't remember the last time somebody paid for *his* meal, much less a young somebody. He looked at me and said "Thank you, Jason" with so much pride in his voice it set my world still for a second.

It wasn't the amount of money involved that made the meal memorable. It wasn't even that I paid, really, because even a debt dope could have put the bill on a credit card. It was my uncle realizing that at least one other person in the family could handle money, that at least one wouldn't be asking for a loan, that at least one could give rather than take.

Financial freedom is yours for the making, no matter what your income. A modest income managed well will create vast reserves of cash as the months go by. A massive income managed wrong will create insolvency as the months go by. It comes down to what you do with your money, so do the right thing and let freedom ring.

CHAPTER 8

Guarantee Your Own Well-Being

For some reason, people think they need to master a thousand little details to properly manage their money. They fret over which credit card incentive program pays back the most for every dollar spent. They compare dozens of bank accounts to find the highest interest rate by 0.01 percent. They study stock charting to day trade between meetings at work. These efforts take up a lot of time and add up to almost no benefit. Following the First Rule of Finance and managing the Three Cs takes up little time and guarantees financial success. Let's review them:

First Rule of Finance: Spend no more than 80 percent of your take-home pay.

Credit cards: Never carry a balance.

Cars: Don't finance. Pay cash for your vehicles.

Castles: Put at least 20 percent down on your house, and keep the mortgage payment below 40 percent of your take-home pay.

Investing Can Wait

Take it from me, an investor, that investing will not do as much for you as swearing to never carry a balance on your credit cards. Do you know what it means to do well in the stock market? Earning an average of 10 percent per year. Do you know what keeping your credit card balance at zero pays? A *guaranteed* 11 to 18 percent per year, or more. Where do you suppose you should focus first?

Without knowing a thing about dividend yields, valuation ratios, earnings growth, market risk, moving averages, retracement levels, wave cycles, or any of the other details of stock investing, you can "beat the market" by simply keeping your credit cards paid off. You didn't know how easy it was to be smart, did you?

There are exceptions, I know, but too many people see exceptions as rules. It reminds me of the saying "The race is not always to the swift, nor the battle to the strong—but that's the way to bet." When emotions fail you, go with the odds. There's always a guy who claims to have made a million on a penny stock last year, and it's possible, but it's not probable. I'd bet my own fortune you'll lose whatever you invest in penny stocks trying to make a million, and I'll get rich while you get poor, driving yourself crazy and mumbling, "But it just *had* to go up."

I publish a newsletter about investing, write books about investing, and give speeches about investing, so you know I believe in it. What I'm pointing out here is that it should not be anybody's *first* priority. We have a name for the first priority, remember? It's easy to know it comes first because it's called the First Rule of Finance. Investing begins several steps down the list, but a lot of people skip the boring first steps in favor of the exciting later steps. "Buy, sell, profit!" beckons loudly, as if it were that easy. It's not, but you know what is? This advice: "Save steadily, stupid!"

Don't devote even 10 seconds to investing until you've mastered the First Rule of Finance and controlled the Three Cs.

It's impossible to overstate how much more important they are than any investment idea to your financial well-being. Investments involve risk, sometimes a lot of risk. They are never guaranteed. Mastering the First Rule and the Three Cs guarantees you a life of financial ease. Let's consider how.

The First Rule guarantees that your savings will increase every month because you'll never spend more than 80 percent of your income. Just by existing, you'll get richer.

Paying off your credit card balance each month guarantees that you'll never pay a dime in interest or late fees, which cost much more than almost any investment pays.

Paying cash for your car guarantees that you won't pay interest, and comes close to guaranteeing that you'll limit yourself to a reasonable price and own the car for as long as possible. All of that guarantees more money in your pocket—something few investments can do.

Putting 20 percent down on a house and getting a mortgage with fixed payments you can afford guarantees that you'll never be homeless. You shouldn't consider your home to be an investment, but if you buy it at a reasonable price it will act as one by appreciating over the long haul. Plus, it's nice to have a place to live. Try finding a stock, bond, mutual fund, or bar of gold that keeps you dry in the rain.

Look at those four financial guarantees. Do you see that no politician, no banker, and no investment advisor can offer as much? They can't guarantee anything, and very often get you into a world of hurt with their latest great ideas. You don't need their great ideas. You don't need anything fancy. You just need what you guarantee *yourself* by following the First Rule and controlling the Three Cs: growing wealth and a wonderfully liberating absence of debt.

If you follow these basics, nobody can get you.

When the fickle Fed and the diabolic banks and the debt dopes played their parts to crater the economy, financially smart people who followed the First Rule and managed the Three Cs were fine. They didn't lose their homes. They didn't worry much about losing their jobs, because their savings could tide them over. It doesn't take long to save enough money to be able to survive a year or more without a job—especially if you're good at budgeting and controlling your need to buy things, skills you'll automatically acquire just by spending less than you earn. See how it all works together?

If you never own a single share of stock in your life, but adhere to the First Rule of Finance and get the Three Cs right, you'll do better than almost any investor who speculates on rising prices while mismanaging the basics.

Besides, if you don't have control of your finances before striking it rich on some investment, what makes you think you will afterwards? No matter how much money you make, if you manage it badly, it will disappear. Get the management part down first when the stakes are low and easy, then you can move up to investing later when you know how to handle money. If you can't handle paying off your credit card each month, you can't handle stocks. First learn money management, then move on to investing, if you want. Don't reverse the order. That's like going to skydiving school and spending all your time studying how to land without ever learning to pull the ripcord. If you don't know how to pull the ripcord, your landing techniques won't help much. Similarly, if you don't know how to manage your money, investment techniques won't help much. In both cases, you're dead.

For back-up on this idea, I turn to a successful investor friend of mine named Charles Kirk in Cedar City, Utah. In addition to trading stocks for a living, Charles runs a popular investment web site called The Kirk Report. He turned a $2,000 trading account into $1 million in 14 years.

You would expect a guy like Charles to urge you to speculate your way to success, right? He doesn't, though. He discussed with his subscribers in August 2009 the subject of building wealth. His rule will sound familiar to you by now: "As for building wealth, it always comes down to a simple rule—through both the good and bad times, you must *always* live well below your means."

There it is, again: the First Rule of Finance.

Charles wrote that he and his wife "try to live on her meager teacher's salary so we can have enough money put aside that we'll be okay no matter what happens in the future. That sacrifice has provided us tremendous comfort and advantages that others simply don't have."

Where did he pick up such a lifestyle? From his parents, who "grew up dirt-poor and taught me the importance of never going into debt and buying things I couldn't already afford. Thinking back through my life, living by this rule has saved me lots of worry and fear and has opened up opportunities that wouldn't have been available to me otherwise."

Indeed. You read in Chapter 4, "Debt is control. If they can keep you in debt, they can control you." People not in debt are not controlled. They live how they want. They live free. Charles has been able to take advantage of opportunities others couldn't pursue because he lives a life of assets while they live a life of debt. He is free, they are enslaved.

Society, you'll do well to remember, is tilted toward financial slavery, not financial freedom. Charles recognizes that. About his lifestyle of living within his family's means and saving for the future, he wrote, "As you know, our American culture doesn't agree with this practice. In fact, it does everything it can to encourage and promote the exact opposite and we've only started to see the impact of this." That impact was the subprime mortgage recession and its aftermath.

Maybe investors, such as Charles, are better equipped than most to see that investing can wait. Nobody knows more about balancing risk and reward than a stock trader. How about a quick recap? Living within your means: no risk, all reward. Keeping your credit card balance at zero: no risk, all reward. Buying stocks: lots of risk, only potential reward. Go with the guarantees.

Too many people watch financial news each day, worried that something is going to explode. As you saw in our traipse down Financial Memory Lane in Chapter 3, they have good reason to worry. Financial systems routinely blow up, and always will. You can't control them. You can't make the Dow Jones Industrial Average go up. You can't make corporations honor their dividend commitments. You can't force Congress to regulate bankers, especially since bankers pay politicians. You can control only your little piece of the financial world.

But you know what? That's enough.

Focus on Your Finances

Get your own finances in order, and you'll be safe. You won't need to worry about the latest goofiness from Washington, the newest Ponzi scheme on Wall Street, whether the Treasury secretary is sending your tax payments directly to Goldman Sachs, or whether the Federal Reserve chairman is a bubble blower. Set your own course in life, and stick to it. If your personal financial house is in order when economic calamity strikes, you'll be in a great position to benefit from the emergency measures. We saw this in the subprime crisis. The Federal Reserve dropped interest rates to near zero, then began buying up long-term Treasuries to drop mortgage rates to below 5 percent. That's cheap, and smart people with cash were able to buy real estate at low prices with low interest rates. The dummies panicked and complained about being victims, but the smarties jumped for joy.

Panic makes for better news than joy, so you didn't read much about the smart people benefiting from the meltdown. Wouldn't you rather have been one of them, though? Imagine sitting on a pile of cash that you saved up over the years. All your bills are paid because you never got in over your head. Your credit card is at a zero balance. You never had a car payment. Your cash is your cash to do with as you please. You notice people losing their jobs and losing their homes, you read that the government is bailing out this bank and that, you see the Fed slashing interest rates to zero, and you see property values crashing. You don't have to be a billionaire to make something of all that. Finding a good property at a newly discounted price and financing it with a mortgage below 5 percent was brilliant. If you already owned a home, you could have bought a second one to rent out. The people able to keep cool and make smart moves during the crisis were the same ones who acted smart before the crisis—and after, for that matter. Once you've experienced

Red Frog Coffee

Another way the recession proved useful to those sitting on solid finances was by offering up commercial space at a song. My sister, Emily, and I had wanted to open a coffee shop together for years—talent from her, capital from me—but never quite found the right opportunity.

The recession blew in and set many corporations on edge. Among them was a little chain of coffee shops you may have heard of named Starbucks. It decided to reduce its store count, and closed its newest shop in Longmont, Colorado, near where Emily and I grew up. Located at the corner of a new outdoor shopping complex, the site enjoys direct signage exposure to 30,000 cars per day driving on Ken Pratt Boulevard.

Under normal circumstances, such a superb site never would have become available to a non-national brand. Because of the recession and Starbucks's restructuring plans, however, the shop not only became available, it did so at one third of what the landlord considered to be fair market value. Plus, it was already built-out by Starbucks to be a coffee shop. That saved Emily and me some $40,000 in construction costs.

You know what enabled us to jump on the opportunity? Smart money management. Had we frittered away our start-up capital on credit card fees, car payments, and bloated mortgages, we wouldn't have been able to open the shop. Financial freedom made it possible.

Because of that, we probably should have called the place Freedom Coffee, but we called it Red Frog Coffee instead. If you're ever in Longmont, stop by for a sip of freedom. Tell the barista I sent you.

the joy of life lived by the First Rule and undamaged by the Three Cs, you won't be able to imagine it any other way. It'll be your default mode, because it's peaceful and easy.

You may not know this yet, but your financial contentment comes more from the direction of your worth than the value. If you get richer with each passing month, you feel pretty good even in the beginning when the growth may be from just $500 to $1,000 to $1,500. A young woman on that path with only $1,500 is not rich this month, but she's richer than she was a month ago and she'll be even better off one month hence. Her future is bright. By contrast, a man with a net worth of $5 million who sees it drop to $4.5 million then $4 million then $3.5 million feels awful. He still has far more money than the young woman, but she's improving with each month while he's deteriorating. She feels good. He doesn't.

The great investor Warren Buffet said that time is the friend of the wonderful company, the enemy of the mediocre. It's the same with people. Time is the friend of the financially intelligent, the enemy of the dull. Smart people see their net worth grow with every passing month as they sock more away in savings, acquire more assets, and make good decisions. Financially stupid people see their situation grow more dire with every passing month, as they spend more than they earn, rack up more debt, and make bad decisions. Some things can't go on forever, and spending $12 for every $10 earned is one of them. Smart people feel good as their wealth grows. Stupid people feel bad as their wealth shrinks.

You know how to guarantee feeling good? Get richer every month. You know how to do that? Follow the First Rule and control the Three Cs. That'll put you on the right track of steadily growing wealth, and you'll find it hard to believe anybody chooses to live another way.

Advertisers sell a bastardized version of the good life. The "get it now" illusion of finding happiness in big houses, big cars, and big spending on debt isn't happiness at all.

Too many people reading the First Rule of Finance and how to control the Three Cs see the plan as boring, too prudent, no fun. They're utterly misguided. Advertisers pull their strings so easily. The irony is that seeking happiness through big houses, big cars, and big spending on debt creates misery. Saving cash and *then* getting the house you want, the car you want, and the lifestyle you want creates true happiness, at least as far as material wealth is concerned.

Society's path of least resistance leads directly to where you *don't* want to be. Institutions have set it up that way because the default destination where most people obligingly end up puts wealth in the pockets of government, banks, and big business. You have to choose your destination, plan how to get there, and then work hard on your plan. You must defend yourself against society being wrong, because it will be wrong for the rest of your life with a few spans of deceptive tranquility along the way.

If you get the First Rule down and the Three Cs right, you'll find your life becoming heaven. You'll enjoy your work more because you'll know you're doing it by choice, not by necessity to service debt. You'll take more vacations and better vacations because you'll have the money to pay for them and you won't need to rush back to work. Good times through borrowing are not good at all. Good times through saving are the only sound currency in our bankrupt world.

From the warm nest of your own financial guarantees, the topsy-turvy, debt-laden, indentured servitude of the average dope looks like madness. It *is* madness. The only reason people don't see it that way is that it's become the accepted norm. Government succeeded in getting most people hooked on paying taxes automatically, banks succeeded in getting most people hooked on debt, and companies succeeded in getting most people hooked on buying everything.

By God, don't let them hook you.

9

On the Front Lines of Freedom

This is no academic treatise. The threats to your money are real, and other people like you are fighting to achieve financial freedom, or guard the freedom they've already achieved. Let's spend time with some of them, see their mistakes, find their solutions, and glean tips that will help you in your own fight. All of the following stories are true, told to me by people on the "free list" at JasonKelly.com.

Jack Chism is a professor of management at Greenville College in Greenville, Illinois. Back in 1982, he spoke about money management to a group of engaged couples. He used his own car-buying history from his then–14 years of marriage to show the true cost of financing new cars. He came up with three numbers for them:

1. $28,000: The total of the car payments he and his wife made in 14 years.
2. $18,000: The total of the sticker prices for the cars they bought.
3. $14,000: The amount they'd have needed to save in high-interest bank accounts (available in the 1970s) to accumulate money to pay cash for the same cars.

So, Jack asked his audience, where did the $10,000 difference between the car payments and the sticker prices go? Everybody knew: the banks. Right, and that plus another $4,000 could have been added to the Chism family balance sheet by *first* saving and *then* buying, which is what they do now. I wish more professors taught lessons like that.

One guy who could have used such a lesson is the unemployed friend of Carlos Cao, who lives in New York City. The friend offered to drive Carlos home after dinner one night, and Carlos was surprised to see him driving a new Mercedes-Benz model that Carlos knew to cost somewhere between $80k and $100k. "How much did you pay for your Benz?" Carlos asked. The friend smiled and said, "I rent it for $500 a month." On top of that, he has to pay car insurance, which is more expensive in New York than in almost any other city in America. All told, the friend is probably paying between $900 and $1,100 per month to drive a car he'll *never* own. Carlos thinks the reason is that he "broke up with his girlfriend a few months ago and wants to look for a new girl using the Benz to attract one." If the new girlfriend costs him that much money before he's even met her, I can't wait to hear about his finances once they start dating. Their first outing will probably involve a chartered jet to Iceland for the weekend. You probably think the lesson here is to be smart about cars. No, it's to date financially stupid people! Don't marry them, of course. Once their money and lines of credit are gone, move on.

While Carlos's friend pays $1,100 per month for a car he'll never own, Tom Hohmeier of Chicago pays himself $250 per month for a car he'll pay cash for in the future. He's 50 years old, and has never financed a car in his life. He told me his simple system: "I pay myself $250 per month for a car fund, keep driving my cars for at least 10 years, then use the fund to buy a new one. Anyone can do this by starting small with a used car to build the fund in their late teens or early twenties. It's the biggest no-brainer." Tom's plan keeps him in pretty decent vehicles. At the end of 10 years of saving $250 per month, his automobile fund is worth more than $30,000 every time he goes car shopping, thanks to compound interest on top of the cash value. For example, even at a modest interest rate of 3 percent, his fund gets up to almost $35,000 in 10 years. Not bad.

Here's a heartbreaker for you that shows just what slime inhabit the world of commerce. Neal Lonky is a doctor in Yorba Linda, California. His twenty-something son was diagnosed with autism, but strives to be independent by working as a clerk, driving a car, and even maintaining his own bank account. He was solicited by educational and job-training firms. Neal told me that when the firms discovered his son's communication handicap, "they would ask for ridiculous 'application' fees that were not charged to other customers. He was also taken advantage of by every Internet scam you can imagine. For example, he had *three* companies checking his credit rating simultaneously, and he was laying out over $200 per month in combined fees to all three companies!" Being proud and independent, Neal's son did not show his parents his credit card bills until he was unable to make even the minimum payment. Neal and his wife were able to recover some of the swindled money and report the cases of fraud, but most of the money was long gone. Neal says the moral of the story is that "the predators don't care who you are, and are merciless."

Therefore, I would add, don't let your guard down for a second. If they'll pinch dollars from a person with autism working to live independently, they'll pinch anybody. Widows, orphans, the disabled, the slightly tired, the inattentive, the carefree, the young, the old, the parents of ten kids, the rich, the poor—it's an equal opportunity heist, so watch your back.

Bankers' Rules

To see how banks follow their own rules in society, consider this story shared with me by my high school buddy, Lee Kilgore, a restaurant owner who still lives in our hometown of Estes Park, Colorado.

During the recession caused by the subprime crisis caused by irresponsible banks and stupid borrowers, Lee kept people employed to "help ensure that we all make it." In 2008, he paid himself only $16,000. Through August 2009, when he contacted me, he'd paid himself only $2,500 for that year. His payroll in July 2009, however, was $81,852. In his words, "A good number of people derive their living from my business that is well run and honestly run. During this economic crisis, I have paid all of my bills, kept my employees employed, and paid my taxes—all on time." How many banks do you suppose we can describe as "well run and honestly run?" Some, but you never know, which is why you have to remain on guard. The financial wizards in government, banks, and big business, along with the masses of financially stupid people, make life hard for all of us.

For instance, how do you suppose Lee was rewarded for his well run, honest operation? With a garnishee summons on one of his employees, a debt dope in over his head. Lee told me, "Even though I had nothing to do with this debt, except for inadvertently employing someone with deficient character, the letter accompanying the summons stated that if I did not comply with the wishes of this law firm, they would seek a judgment against me. The letter also stated that I could not terminate the employment of the person being garnished without legal consequences."

The bank was Capital One. Its slogan when Lee contacted me was, "What's in your wallet?" and I suppose the unmentioned second half should have been, "We want it!" Capitol One is one of the ten largest banks in the United States based on deposits. It has nearly 50 million customers, is part of the Fortune 500, and is listed on the New York Stock Exchange under the symbol COF. In November 2008, it received $3.6 billion from taxpayers via the Treasury's Capital Purchase Program (CPP), which was part of the $700-billion Troubled Asset Relief Program (TARP) you read about earlier.

About such a bank forcing him to collect from a dead-beat debtor, Lee fumed, "So, not only am I paying to keep a bad bank in business through my taxes, I am paying for their lawyers to hold me responsible for the collection of their irresponsible lending. My business has to spend extra time and money every week to collect their debt for them, even after we bailed them out."

What fine friends we have in banking!

Sometimes people from outside of America's culture of debt bring a helpful perspective on how life can be lived. Sarp Yeletaysi is one of them. He came to the United States from Turkey for graduate school and to work in Arlington, Virginia. During his first seven years in the country, he looked around at the way people lived and asked friends how the United States could sustain such a high standard of living and consumption given its much lower rate of production. The answer was debt, but it never made sense to Sarp. He became part of American society without buying into the economic manipulations. He told me that the rational part of him rejected "the financial ideas being pumped into the society on a daily basis. Credit cards and debt were advertised almost as if they were good, risk-free things. Carrying a balance on your credit card was advertised as if you will never be asked to pay that *and* the interest back. People were being encouraged to drive bigger cars, SUVs, via tax breaks and, in fact, until very recently the U.S. car manufacturers did not even seem to care to produce small efficient cars like those in Europe."

He noticed people he knew buying "big and expensive houses that they didn't really need" and which "they could not properly afford, by which I mean they did not take into account their (nonexistent) savings and risks of losing a job." The central problem as he saw it: "Having savings is not encouraged in this country. Contrary to that, people are encouraged to spend more than what they make using credit cards and loans." Sarp decided that instead of amassing debt, he'd create savings and investments for himself, and came up with a plan to survive America's debt-based financial environment:

- He watches almost no TV in order to "avoid stupid commercials" that lead viewers into making money mistakes. He uses the time saved for more productive activities.
- He reads about financial issues and discusses them with others, but makes his own decisions after careful consideration.
- He lives within his means by spending no more than he earns. He thinks growing up in "a relatively mid-income country and knowing that it is doable and you can still be happy, is helpful in that matter."
- He has driven the same small, efficient pre-owned car for years.
- He tries to save money every month, and succeeds "90 percent of the time."

Some of those ideas will look familiar to you by now. I was happy to see something like the First Rule of Finance among Sarp's habits. Looking over his financial ideas, is there any doubt that he's a man getting wealthier with each passing month? His life is his own, lived his way, debt-free and wide open to whatever future he wants to make.

Fighting the Fed

Along with everybody else in this chapter, you have to fight the Federal Reserve and America's culture of debt to break free, as shown in the following excerpt from Ron Paul's book, *End the Fed*:

Artificially low interest rates are achieved by inflating the money supply, and they penalize the thrifty and cheat those who save. They promote consumption and borrowing over saving and investing.

Manipulating interest rates is an immoral act. It's economically destructive.

The Fed encourages irresponsible accumulation of personal debt. People live beyond their means with the help of an expansionist monetary policy. They trade in their futures for the present. They neglect the need to save in order to consume more and more. In this sense, the Fed is the ultimate promoter of consumerism and living for the present. This amounts to a terrible cultural distortion in which short-term thinking wins out over long-term planning.

Free Families

Another man who shows that it's possible to break free is Andrew Crawford, a 37-year-old father of five with a stay-at-home wife. They live in Los Angeles. The family income is only what he creates as a computer programmer. He's always lived on 80 percent of that income and carries no credit card debt.

Thanks to such careful money management, he was able to buy a 900-square-foot fixer-upper that nobody else wanted when he was 27 years old. He described the house to me as "a real dump, but one of the only homes that I could afford." That's why he paid just $133,000 for it. He and his wife fixed it up themselves and sold it four years later for triple the price they paid, then used the proceeds to move into a four-bedroom "delight" just "a little up the freeway, for the same price." He got a mortgage on that place with a low 4.8 percent interest rate. His monthly payment uses just 20 percent of his monthly income. Here's a man who's earned the right to brag about his finances, so let's give him the floor:

> I carry no credit card debt, I pay off my credit card at the end of every month. Other than my house, I carry no long-term debt except a minivan payment—I have

a paid-off 10-year-old Mazda MPV minivan and a 2006 Toyota Sienna minivan [on which] I put 10k down, the loan is five years at 0 percent, so my car monthlies are a manageable $280. Yeah, that's right, with five kids, I'm a two-minivan family. [However,] the Mazda sits mostly unused as I commute the 10 miles each way to work on my bicycle, [for] which my employer pays me $2 per day; factor in gas savings and it works out to about 80 bucks a month back into my pocket. I don't take flashy vacations or eat out at restaurants very often, but I feel that's the price for the life I want, a nice family life within my financial means. It's worth every penny!

Oh, to have a few more families like that in America. How far do you think bank shenanigans and corporate tomfoolery will get with Andrew? Not very far. You'll never find him signed on to a crazy loan, sending credit card interest to a bank, sending car loan interest to another bank, mortgaged to his eyeballs, or rushing off to the mall to get five pairs of $100 shoes for his kids. Around responsibility such as Andrew's, the banking and big business fraud that has nearly bankrupted the country wouldn't have wrapped even one tentacle.

Like Andrew's family, Darin Grant's family has its financial act together. They live in Thornton, Colorado, a suburb of Denver. You met Darin's father, Richard Grant, in Chapter 7. When Richard and his wife hit hard times, they moved in with Darin to get back on their feet. If not for Darin's healthy finances, he would have been in no position to help his father and stepmother. Those healthy finances were no accident. They emerged from years of smart money decisions.

Living below their means comes naturally to the Grants. They find the best vacation deals online, and also buy their electronic goods online to get better prices and avoid sales tax. When it comes to shopping with credit cards, the family philosophy is simple: "We still go out and spend money on things that are important to us, but if we don't have the cash to pay off the credit cards before finance charges, we don't go."

Remember early in the book when you read that using credit card point systems properly puts the joke on the bank? The Grants have that tactic down cold. They channel as much of their spending through their credit card as possible to accrue points. The one they use rewards them with a $250 check when they've accrued 200 points. "We cash at least four of these in a year," Darin told me. "How many other people do you know who don't have annual fees, don't pay any finance charges, and have their credit cards *pay them*?" Not many, I'm afraid, but I hope to know more among the readers of this book. You, perhaps?

The car scene at the Grant house looks healthy, too. Darin's wife drives a 2002 Saturn sedan that she initially financed to get some credit history. However, she paid it off just 14 months later, and it was a dealer demo that cost only $14k, versus the $18k sticker price. Darin drives a 1999 Lexus RX300 AWD that he bought in late 2001 as a lease return. That shaved $10k off the $37k sticker price, so he paid only $27k. Like his wife, he financed but paid the car off early. He says the Lexus was a bit of a splurge, but because he and his wife are avid skiers, they "appreciate the stability and reliability for trips into the mountains and the occasional blizzard in the Denver metro area." He plans to drive that Lexus for a while because "the longer I keep it, the cheaper it is to own." Money that most families would be putting toward car payments, the Grants put away as savings so they can buy future vehicles with cash. Way to go!

Knowing what you now know of the Grants, what do you suppose their housing picture looks like? Do you think they put nothing down on a home they couldn't afford, and financed it with a no-doc liar's loan sporting an adjustable interest rate that doubled from payment 25 on? Do you think I know about them because they found themselves upside down in the crisis, crushed by a home worth less than the value of its mortgage, rushing to a public shelter carrying a week-old infant dusted in Denver snowflakes? Not on your life. Smart is their operating word, and here's how it guided their home purchase.

In 2004, they bid on a foreclosed home in Henderson, another Denver suburb. It was built in late 2001 and had an appraised value of $200k. They bid $180k and asked the government to pay closing costs. They won the auction and came away with an instant $20k in equity. Then, they directed as much of their free cash toward that mortgage as possible, getting it down to a balance of only $60k in 2009. They plan to pay it off entirely by 2013.

While most of their neighbors slipped under water, the Grants took advantage of the housing market downturn. They found a new Meritage Homes house in Thornton with an initial price of $390k in a neighborhood with good schools and convenient access to shopping centers and major highways. After some dickering with Meritage, the Grants bought the home for $335k plus closing costs with a 30-year fixed-rate mortgage at 4.5 percent. Of course, they put 20 percent down. At $1,700 per month, their payment is only $400 more than it had been at their other home in Henderson, which they turned into a rental property to create more cash flow. By the way, what do you suppose their neighbors in Thornton paid for comparable homes? At least one ponied up $409k, and probably at a higher interest rate, too.

The Grants show how it's done. Step by step, financially smart people fill their lives with assets that grow their wealth over time. Financially stupid people fill their lives with depreciating trifles that smother them in debt over time. Be like the Grants. Be smart.

Bud's Credit Card War

Fifty-one-year-old Bud Garofalo of New York received several mailings per week from credit card companies offering him zero percent financing on balance transfers and cash advances. He didn't carry a balance or need cash, so he never gave the offers a thought until one day his friend reported owing Citibank more in interest expense than he could ever repay. Bud made a personal loan to his friend to cover the debt, then launched a war against credit card companies.

Touting his excellent credit rating, Bud asked credit card company supervisors to raise his limits. He got two cards up to $50k, and others up to $30k. For a measly $35 fee in some cases, free in others, he controlled a total of $200k of credit card company cash. He deposited the cash in his bank at interest, set up automatic minimum payments on the cards from the bank account, and watched the bank account balance grow as the interest accrued outpaced the minimum payments. He cleared almost $7,000 the first year, enough to pay his school and property taxes.

"Discover made the silliest offer," he told me. "They charged zero percent interest for 12 months, then required just a $25 purchase each month to keep the balance interest-free for three years or until the loan was paid back."

Bud prepared to cover the balances in full when the zero percent financing ended, but to his disbelief Discover made him the same offer again. For a $35 fee, Bud received from Discover another $50k cash at zero interest.

With a spreadsheet and careful planning, Bud never made the mistakes the credit card companies expected him to make. He danced around their traps and made out like a bandit.

Dream Daughter

Laura Reynold and her husband managed their finances the right way from the get-go. They met in Southern California about 20 years ago. Upon graduating from college, she had *no* student loan debt (no wonder he married her) and he had only a little (but it was balanced out by his dashing good looks). Lest you think Laura's degree was financed by rich parents, I should mention that she paid for her own education by working hard in high school and winning scholarships. What wouldn't you give for a daughter like that?

Laura is one smart cookie, an observation I make for several reasons, not least of which is that she waited for her husband to pay off his student loan debt before she accepted his marriage proposal. He went on to get his MBA, but they made sure his company footed that bill. Thus on a financially clean slate, they walked down the aisle at a small 50-person gathering and combined their savings with the money that would have gone toward a sumptuous ceremony into a down payment on their first home. They turned the condominium where he'd lived before the wedding into a rental property. Laura remembers that having both properties "was a stretch at first, but after two or three years we were fine, cash-flow wise." You know why? Because they forwent "expensive vacations and new cars during that period." No keeping up with the Jones jerks for them!

Shortly after that, they argued over whether or not to pay down their new home mortgage early. Her husband wanted to pay it down; Laura wanted to stick with the bank's schedule. That MBA was worth something, because he's correct that paying down early was a good move for the family finances. Laura told me, "I'm now a convert—my husband was so right on this one! We paid off our home balance in just under five years and then paid off the condo in another two years. This is Southern California real estate we're talking about, so the amounts were fairly high." That means it took a lot of scrimping and saving, wrought-iron discipline in a world of trifle advertisements and crafty banking ploys and bought-off government spending of tax money on activities that fatten corporations but don't benefit citizens. The Reynolds stuck to their financial guns through the societal assault on their wealth-building efforts, and they won.

How they won wasn't hard, but the guts to follow their path are hard to come by. Here's how Laura describes their financial habits: "We have always paid off our credit cards monthly, and just use them to get frequent-flyer miles. We have also saved first for our retirement, and those accounts we believe will be adequate for what we hope will be a long life."

They moved north to Silicon Valley. Instead of buying a modern-day castle, of which there are many in that area, they bought a small two-bedroom place. Doing so enabled them to keep their home and condo in Southern California as rental properties. That small sacrifice paid off, too. Laura reports, "We have since 'traded up' into a larger home, and continued the same practice of paying down the mortgage early."

Now, on top of that financial foundation they built through sacrifice and smart money management, they're able to live a more opulent lifestyle without relying on debt to pay for it. "Cars and vacations and saving for college have come more easily in the last five or six years as my husband's career has grown," Laura told me. "I now have the luxury of staying home with our 13-year-old."

What has the journey taught her? That living within one's means is critical. She says it's the "mantra my family has practiced rigorously." Looking back, she recalls that "on our salaries, especially when I was working, we could have bought luxury cars and had personal trainers, but we didn't. We have always bought new cars, but we keep them for eight or nine years. We've only financed one, which was a very good deal."

The recession brought on by bad bankers tricking financially stupid people didn't faze the Reynolds. Laura wrote me in September 2009, "Even in this environment, we have peace of mind because we have assets and no debt. Our challenge is to instill this lifestyle in our son. We're working on that." I bet they'll succeed, too. What a lucky kid he is to have parents like that, and what a stronger nation we'd be if more families lived like the Reynolds.

A Warmly Lit House

In Chapter 3, you read the story of one big bank's subprime equity credit card division as shared with me by Aaron Sweyne, who worked there for 15 years before the bank closed the division in the credit crisis. Recall that toward the end of his career in 2007, Aaron had finally had enough of the business of getting people into debt and wanted to tell every customer, "Stop borrowing money, spend less than you make, get an emergency fund saved up, get out of debt, and *then* you will succeed financially."

Aaron has seen the debt monster from several sides. He's been a borrower, and he's been a bank employee selling debt to customers. He's seen debt used wisely to invest in the future, and he's seen it used disastrously to fund a life filled with depreciating trifles. Despite his working in the trenches of debt creation, he and his family were themselves snagged by the trap of borrowing and spending.

He told me in August 2009, "Four years ago, my wife Sue and I were not extravagant spenders compared to some of our friends, but we did get caught up in the 'buy now, pay later' lifestyle. We frequently traded cars, we sometimes charged our vacations on the credit card, and my wife was a pretty avid clothes and decorations shopper. Plus, we had two small kids who seemed to need everything all the time. We both worked hard at good-paying jobs, and together we made over $125,000 in 2005."

The problem was, they hated those good-paying jobs. Because of the borrow-to-buy trap that had snapped on their lives, however, they couldn't easily quit their jobs. Sue saw a way out. "She wanted to do something she felt passionate about," Aaron wrote, "instead of sitting in a cubicle working customer service for a transportation company." Sue had a knack for floral design and worked a few weddings on the side. She thought she could start a retail flower shop to make money doing something that made her happy. It's not easy pursuing a dream, though, as she and Aaron quickly discovered.

He recalled, "We needed about $20,000 in start-up money to get the business going. At the time, we owed about $25,000 on two cars and another $5,000 on a credit card. It was an unbelievably stressful time for us—we had always made enough money to pay our debts, but now we were going to cut our income by 35 percent, take on more debt, and venture into the uncertainty of self-employment. We almost didn't do it. I did not think we could afford it. Sue and I went back and forth; she believed she could do it, so I gave in."

What came next was a complete financial transformation of their family. A lovely by-product of properly managing debt is that the rest of a person's or family's financial picture automatically improves. A debt-smart person is a money-smart person, almost without fail. Those who get debt under control get the rest of their financial life under control, too. Here's how it happened to Aaron and Sue, in Aaron's words: "We traded down in cars, we cut out vacations, and we generally scaled back our lifestyle and focused all extra money on paying off debt. Ironically, focusing on paying off debt simultaneously gets you focused on making more money, saving more money, and investing. It has been a lot of work, but the business is on the path to success. She is paying herself a small salary, paying her employees and all her monthly bills with cash-flow from the business, and is now starting to pile up some cash in the business account. But most importantly, we have *no debt* and are on the path for steady growth in profit. I feel really fortunate that my initial doubts were wrong."

Aaron and Sue's story looks like the only warmly lit house filled with laughter on a long street lined with dark, slumping buildings inhabited by debt dopes. Their neighbors shuffle out the door each morning to jobs they hate to service the crushing debt on their shoulders, and they can't get out. At least, most never will. Maybe a few others will make the same leap that took Aaron and Sue from owing to owning, but the majority will live their lives as societal pawns.

Aaron considers the First Rule of Finance and control of the Three Cs to be "so important," and here's why: "When you want to make a change in your life, take a risk, or simply take advantage of an opportunity, debt is an anchor that weighs you down and limits your options."

Avoid the Door of Despondency

It's the snuffing of freedom that makes debt so harmful to happiness. When you borrow to buy things that depreciate, you knock on the door of despondency.

You now know how to avoid that door, even in America's debt-based society. Smart money management whisks you past the door, down the hallway, and into the light of living joyfully however and wherever you'd like. Set your sights on freedom. Leap over the tripwires stretched by government, banks, and big business. Dash to the life you want.

You'll wonder what took you so long.

In Yourself You Trust

You might have found this book rude in parts, but it had to be. Other financial writers and I have written politely and thoroughly on this subject for years—to no avail. The mindless consumption continued, lending and borrowing entered Wonderland when debtors didn't even need to prove their ability to repay, and the entire economy caught fire because of it. Tough times call for tough medicine, so writing the same prudent 400 tips for financial health in the same gentle tones wouldn't cut it. Nobody followed these tips before; why would they now? A smack upside the head was in order, and this book is it. It's short enough to cover all that matters, and it punches hard and straight in hopes of finally knocking some sense into a few noggins.

You and I covered a lot of ground together.

We learned that the basics of money management are pretty darned easy, and that there's no excuse for people getting them wrong. We learned that people got them wrong anyway, then claimed to be victims and demanded handouts. We learned that government, banks, and speculators have a long history of blowing up the financial system, but people still expect sensible rules and regulations from them. We learned that the entire country is built on a culture of debt, from the government to banks to big business to credit card crackheads who still haven't figured out that financing a pair of sneakers at 18 percent isn't smart.

We saw that the banks of the Federal Reserve encourage people to borrow and spend by constantly expanding the money supply. That puts cash everywhere and makes savings lose value over time. Easy credit slips fast money into the hands of people who use it to buy depreciating trifles. The price of trifles goes up and so does the debt amassed to buy them at the higher prices. The bought trifles lose value while the debt load that bought them grows from interest expenses. Banks lending money are happy. Companies selling trifles are happy. Idiots swapping rising debt for cheapening trifles are miserable, and don't even know why.

We realized that from the moment of our birth we're operating on a low financial battery. Government is owned by corporations, so most of the money you pay in taxes is wasted on spending for programs that benefit corporations instead of you, such as bailouts and bombs. One third of your money is blown on that kind of stuff, which means you have to spend money to buy the things that your taxes don't buy for you, such as health insurance, higher education, and car insurance. Those items chew through another third of your money. That's how, from the get-go, only about one third of your income landed within your control. If you screw up managing that third—and most people do—there's nothing but indentured servitude in your future.

Financial people are everywhere in society's leadership positions, manipulating the legal and cultural environment to direct money to themselves. Financially stupid people are everywhere in the populace, confused by the wily ruses used to get their money, and opening wide for the lures dangled before them.

We learned that government, banks, and big business like it that way. Debt makes a wonderful trap for keeping people dutifully showing up at jobs to service their loans, pay their taxes, and buy more things they don't need. Debt-free people live free, move where *they* want, work how *they* want, and are generally not right where the big institutions want them to be. They're where *they* want to be, and that's freedom.

Banks are predators. Government is incompetent at best, complicit at worst. Companies want to sell you this year's trifles by saying they're better than last year's—though not as good as next year's, mind you. Most of your neighbors, relatives, and coworkers long ago fell into the trap of borrowing and spending. They're all lost causes. There's nobody to look out for you, except . . . you, my friend. There's only you.

The good news is, you're enough.

You can do it. Your own two feet are the best you'll ever find for standing tall and walking proud through the forest of billboards, blinking online ads, flashing TVs, blaring radios, and chattering dunderheads all telling you to buy, buy, buy. You'll smile as the cacophony of a society in debt turns to meaningless banter because you hear your own clear tone. It's the ring of a bell at first light. You'll buy what *you* want to buy when *you* want to buy it with money *you've* saved from *your* income. That's all. Nothing more. Nobody will ever tell you what or when or how to buy, ever again.

Within that cone of silence, you'll find yourself. You'll realize that you can set your own course and even pace your progress along it toward the places you want to go, the way you want to live. The dangers will disappear as your destination fills the horizon. Unencumbered, you'll look up one day and say, "This is my time on Earth, and I can do anything I want with it."

You read at the beginning of this book that the nature of your whole life comes down to how you answer one question: Will I live in debt or will I live free? I hope you live free.

Once you choose to live free, you need only master the First Rule of Finance and control the Three Cs. They are:

First Rule of Finance: Spend no more than 80 percent of your take-home pay.

Credit cards: Never carry a balance.

Cars: Don't finance. Pay cash for your vehicles.

Castles: Put at least 20 percent down on your house, and keep the mortgage payment below 40 percent of your take-home pay.

There's not a lot to it. Get it right, and you'll be free.

A

Smart Scenarios

Here's a cheat sheet to help you leave financially stupid people in the dust as you race toward freedom. It shows the First Rule of Finance and control of the Three Cs for various levels of monthly take-home pay. Follow these guidelines to avoid the pitfalls of inflation sponsored by the Federal Reserve, limit the damage done by government's wasteful spending for the benefit of its corporate owners, escape predatory bankers, and laugh at big business marketing tricks.

If Your Monthly Take-Home Pay Is	You Can Spend Up to 80%, Which Is	You'll Save at Least 20%, Which Is	In 5 Years You'll Have Saved at Least	The Balance You'll Carry on Your Credit Card Will Be	Your Car Payment Will Be	Your Mortgage Payment Will Be No More Than 40%, Which Is
$1,000	$800	$200	$12,000	$0	$0	$400
$1,500	$1,200	$300	$18,000	$0	$0	$600
$2,000	$1,600	$400	$24,000	$0	$0	$800
$2,500	$2,000	$500	$30,000	$0	$0	$1,000
$3,000	$2,400	$600	$36,000	$0	$0	$1,200
$3,500	$2,800	$700	$42,000	$0	$0	$1,400
$4,000	$3,200	$800	$48,000	$0	$0	$1,600
$4,500	$3,600	$900	$54,000	$0	$0	$1,800
$5,000	$4,000	$1,000	$60,000	$0	$0	$2,000
$10,000	$8,000	$2,000	$120,000	$0	$0	$4,000
$15,000	$12,000	$3,000	$180,000	$0	$0	$6,000
$20,000	$16,000	$4,000	$240,000	$0	$0	$8,000
$50,000	$40,000	$10,000	$600,000	$0	$0	$20,000
$100,000	$80,000	$20,000	$1,200,000	$0	$0	$40,000
$1,000,000	$800,000	$200,000	$12,000,000	$0	$0	$400,000

APPENDIX B

Getting Out of Debt

If society already caught you in its debt trap, you need to get out as soon as possible. Here are 10 steps for doing so.

1. Discuss the ideas in this book with your family. Get everybody in agreement that it's time to stop living in a way that benefits government, banks, and big business. It's time to live free, and that requires swimming upstream.

2. Using credit card statements, bank statements, receipts, and memory, make a list of your typical monthly expenditures. Look carefully at it with your family, and cut it to the bone. Be ruthless in eliminating unnecessary spending to free up as much cash as possible.

3. Consider who can take on extra income-producing activities, such as part-time jobs, side businesses, profitable hobbies, or overtime at existing jobs.

4. Write down how much extra cash you'll have available after cutting expenses and boosting income.

5. Make a list of your debts in order from smallest to biggest and note each one's minimum monthly payment. Add up the minimums to see how much you need to pay each month to service your debt.

6. Consider which debts you can reduce dramatically or eliminate. For example, you might have financed a new car with unreasonably high payments. How about selling it, paying off the debt entirely, and then getting a cheaper car or no car at all for a while? You may be able to do the same thing with other expensive items you financed.

7. Look at the extra cash you created by cutting expenses and boosting income, the reduced debt load you created by reducing or eliminating some accounts, and the total of all your minimum monthly payments remaining. If you have enough cash each month to cover the minimums and still have some left, great! Pay the minimums and use the extra cash to build a reserve of $1,000. Once you've set aside that $1,000 for emergencies, stop saving into that fund and start directing your extra cash toward paying off your smallest debt entirely. Once that account is paid off, focus your extra cash on the next smallest one, and so on until all of your debt except your mortgage is paid off. Paying off small debts first is called the debt snowball method. For most people, it's better than focusing on biggest debts or highest-interest debts first, because the satisfaction of eliminating accounts from their list encourages them to keep going. Visible progress comes more quickly with the debt snowball approach, and a lot of people need to see that progress. However, if you do not require such encouragement, then reprioritize your debts from highest interest rate to lowest, and pay them off in that order. It'll leave more money in your pocket when you've paid off all the accounts. Destination is more important than detail in this case, so do whatever works for you to kill your debt.

8. If you reduced all the expenses you can, are doing all you can to boost income, and reduced or eliminated all the debts you could, but still don't have enough cash to make your minimum payments, it's

time to smash the emergency glass. Call every one of your creditors and explain your situation to see if they can help. If that doesn't get you anywhere, *carefully* look into debt consolidation loans. Be extremely alert because that field is filled with the very swindlers you're trying to escape, and many of them will slap on high fees and tricky interest rates that may put you farther behind. Also, be careful that you don't make things worse by collateralizing all your consumer debt with your house—and then losing the house if you can't keep up with payments. If none of that helps, you may need to declare bankruptcy. Don't feel too bad. You might see the U.S. Treasury secretary down at bankruptcy court, because the whole country seems headed there.

9. As you pay off credit card accounts, close them until you have just one left. That's all you need, and you'll never carry a balance again.

10. If that one credit card causes problems or you just get tired of paying another bill every month, switch to a debit card. It offers the same convenience and same ability to buy things online and over the phone, yet produces no monthly bill or risk of interest expenses and late fees. It pulls cash directly from your bank account. Financially smart people keep cash in their bank accounts—and you're going to be one of them.

APPENDIX C

Keep Current

The backdrop never changes. Society consists of financial people at the top manipulating financially stupid people below. What does change, however, are the details.

As I wrote this book in 2009, fresh evidence appeared weekly. I'd find a perfect quote in April, only to discover a better one in August, which would end up being replaced in November. Eventually, though, I delivered the book to John Wiley & Sons, sporting the best evidence at hand, in the waning days of 2009.

Unfinished business at that time included the final product of the health care reform effort, the fate of new electric cars, progress in the Afghanistan and Iraq wars, the consequences of America's still-rising debt, and the pace of economic recovery.

If you'd like to receive periodic updates on these and other issues related to achieving financial freedom in a debt-based society, please put yourself on my "free list" at JasonKelly.com. You'll join me and thousands of other people who are deftly defying the borrowing-and-spending trap. It's nice to have a few friends on the front lines of freedom.

I also offer some of the updates specific to this title by including page number references. That way, you can see exactly where new information fits in.

See you soon at JasonKelly.com!

Notes

Chapter 3: Toxic FSP in the Alphabet of Idiocy

1. John Cassidy, "Harder Times," *New Yorker*, March 16, 2009, www.newyorker
.com/talk/comment/2009/03/16/090316taco_talk_cassidy.

Chapter 4: The Society You're Up Against

1. Paul O'Neill, "Ten Trillion and Counting," *Frontline* interview,
November 24, 2008, www.pbs.org/wgbh/pages/frontline/tentrillion/
interviews/oneill.html.
2. Charles A. Lindbergh, *Congressional Record* 51: 1446 (December 22,
1913), with additional comments made after the passage of the Federal
Reserve Act of 1913.
3. Ron Paul, *End the Fed* (New York: Grand Central Publishing, 2009).
4. Ibid.
5. Elizabeth Warren, "Voices of Power," *Washington Post* interview,
October 8, 2009, www.washingtonpost.com/wp-dyn/content/article/
2009/10/08/AR2009100800778.html.

Chapter 5: Government of the Corporations, by the Corporations, for the Corporations

1. William K. Black, *Bill Moyers Journal* interview, April 3, 2009, www.pbs
.org/moyers/journal/04032009/transcript3.html.
2. Gretchen Morgenson, "Revisiting a Fed Waltz with A.I.G," *New York
Times*, November 21, 2009, www.nytimes.com/2009/11/22/business/
22gret.html.
3. Brooksley E. Born, "Prophet and Loss," *Stanford Magazine* profile,
March/April 2009, www.stanfordalumni.org/news/magazine/2009/
marapr/features/born.html.

4. Neil Irwin, "N.Y. Fed Chooses Continuity in Selecting Geithner's Replacement," *Washington Post*, January 27, 2009, www.washingtonpost .com/wp-dyn/content/article/2009/01/27/AR2009012701498.html.

5. Bob Cusack, "Lobbyists Gain Upper Hand in Obama Battle," *The Hill*, July 27, 2009, thehill.com/business-a-lobbying/52295-lobbyists-gain-upper-hand-in-obama-battle.

6. Daniel Stone, "The Browning of Grassroots," *Newsweek* web exclusive, August 20, 2009, www.newsweek.com/id/212934.

7. Matt Taibbi, "The Great American Bubble Machine," *Rolling Stone*, July 9–23,www.rollingstone.com/politics/story/29127316/the_great_ american_bubble_machine.

8. George Friedman, "Obama's Foreign Policy: The End of the Beginning," *Stratfor*, August 24, 2009, www.stratfor.com/weekly/20090824_ obamas_foreign_policy_end_beginning.

9. Peter Baker, "Obama's Pledge to Reform Ethics Faces an Early Test," *New York Times*, February 2, 2009, www.nytimes.com/2009/02/03/us/ politics/03lobby.html.

10. Manuel Roig-Franzia, "Heather Podesta, the Insider's Insider," *Washington Post*, August 24, 2009, www.washingtonpost.com/wp-dyn/ content/article/2009/08/23/AR2009082302381.html.

11. George Carlin, January 2006 HBO special, *"Life Is Worth Losing."*

Chapter 6: How Money Is Power

1. "The Path to a High Performance U.S. Health System: A 2020 Vision and the Policies to Pave the Way," The Commonwealth Fund, February 19, 2009, www.commonwealthfund.org/Content/Publications/Fund-Reports/2009/Feb/The-Path-to-a-High-Performance-US-Health-System.aspx.

2. "Health Spending in the United States and the Rest of the Industrialized World," The Commonwealth Fund, July 12, 2005, www .commonwealthfund.org/Content/Publications/In-the-Literature/ 2005/Jul/Health-Spending-in-the-United-States-and-the-Rest-of-the-Industrialized-World.aspx.

3. "Meeting Enrollees' Needs: How Do Medicare and Employer Coverage Stack Up?," The Commonwealth Fund, May 12, 2009, www .commonwealthfund.org/Content/Publications/In-the-Literature/ 2009/May/Meeting-Enrollees-Needs.aspx.

4. "Senator Bernie Sanders on Healthcare Reform," *Ring of Fire Radio*, June 10, 2009, www.ringoffireradio.com/BlogEngine/post/Senator-Bernie-Sanders-on-Healthcare-Reform.aspx.

5. Betsy McCaughey, *The Fred Thompson Show*, July 16, 2009. No archive is available at the show's site, but there's a good discussion and fact-check

Notes

of it at www.politifact.com/truth-o-meter/statements/2009/jul/23/
betsy-mccaughey/mccaughey-claims-end-life-counseling-will-be-requi/.

6. "How House Bill Runs over Grandma," *Investor's Business Daily*,
July 31, 2009, www.investors.com/NewsAndAnalysis/Article.aspx?
id=503058. The original, faulty version has been replaced with a cor-
rected one, but the reader comment section below the article keeps
the record straight.

7. Bill Hogan, "Pulling Strings from Afar," *AARP Bulletin Today*, July 3,
2006, http://bulletin.aarp.org/yourworld/politics/articles/pulling
_strings_from.html.

8. Bob MacGuffie, "Rocking the Town Halls—Best Practices," *Right
Principles*, undated, but reported on a May 2009 event and distributed
in June 2009, http://thinkprogress.org/wp-content/uploads/2009/
07/townhallactionmemo.pdf.

9. Andrew Weil, "Dr. Andrew Weil on Health Care Reform," *Larry
King Live* (September 10, 2009). http://transcripts.cnn.com/
TRANSCRIPTS/0909/10/lkl.01.html.

10. Wendell Potter. Testimony before the U.S. Senate Committee on
Commerce, Science and Transportation, June 24, 2009, http://com
merce.senate.gov/public/_files/PotterTestimonyConsumerHealth
Insurance.pdf.

11. Bill Moyers, *Bill Moyers Journal* comment, October 9, 2009, www.pbs
.org/moyers/journal/10092009/transcript4.html.

12. Dennis J. Kucinich, "Why I Voted No," November 7, 2009, http://
kucinich.house.gov/NEWS/DocumentSingle.aspx?DocumentID=
153995. Despite his misgivings about the health care reform bill, Kucinich
changed his "no" vote to a "yes" on March 21, 2010. He stopped calling
it "a bailout under a blue cross" that will "lead to even more costs, more
subsidies, and higher profits for insurance companies." He defended his
switch, explaining that "even though I don't like the bill, I've made a decision to support it in the hopes that we can move towards a more compre-
hensive approach once this legislation is done." Notice who called the
shots. The health insurance lobby succeeded in getting votes from politicians who strongly, publicly opposed the ways of its clients, and a new law
passed mandating Americans to buy private health insurance from them.
How's that for a corporate profit booster?

13. Scott DeCarlo, "The World's Biggest Companies," *Forbes*, April 8, 2009,
www.forbes.com/2009/04/08/worlds-largest-companies-business-
global-09-global_land.html.

14. David L. Modisette, "The Current and Future Market for Electric
Vehicles," California Electric Transportation Coalition (CalETC) survey, July 2000. A report on the survey, dated September 7, 2000, is at
www.greencargroup.com/news_newcarbuyers.html.

Notes

15. David Calef and Robert Goble, "The Allure of Technology: How France and California Promoted Electric Vehicles to Reduce Urban Air Pollution," *FEEM Working Paper*, No. 07.05, January, 2005, http://ssrn.com/abstract=650041 or doi:10.2139/ssrn.650041.

16. Arnaud De Borchgrave, "Release Lubricated by Oil," *Washington Times*, August 31, 2009, www.washingtontimes.com/news/2009/aug/31/release-lubricated-by-oil/.

17. Stephen Glover, "The Release of Megrahi for Commercial Reasons Is a Vintage Labour Scandal," *Mail Online*, September 2, 2009, www.dailymail.co.uk/debate/article-1210164/The-release-Megrahi-commercial-reasons-vintage-Labour-scandal.html.

18. Robert Scheer, "Indefensible Spending," *Los Angeles Times*, (June 1, 2008, www.latimes.com/news/opinion/commentary/la-op-scheer1-2008jun01,0,5177531.story.

19. Richard L. Berke, "Lobbying Steps Up on Military Buying as Budget Shrinks," *New York Times*, April 9, 1990, www.nytimes.com/1990/04/09/us/lobbying-steps-up-on-military-buying-as-budget-shrinks.html.

20. Robert M. Gates, "A Balanced Strategy: Reprogramming the Pentagon for a New Age," *Foreign Affairs*, January/February 2009, www.foreignaffairs.com/articles/63717/robert-m-gates/a-balanced-strategy.

21. Matthew P. Hoh, Resignation letter written to Ambassador Nancy J. Powell, Director General of the Foreign Service and Director of Human Resources, September 10, 2009, www.docstoc.com/docs/13944018/Matthew-Hoh-Resignation-Letter.

22. Bob Herbert, "A Tragic Mistake," *New York Times*, November 30, 2009, www.nytimes.com/2009/12/01/opinion/01herbert.html.

23. Barney Frank, "Cut the Military Budget—II," *The Nation* (February 11, 2009). www.thenation.com/doc/20090302/frank.

24. Siobhan Hughes and Brody Mullins, "Emanuel Pick Underscores Balancing Act ahead in Reshaping Financial Industry," *Wall Street Journal*, November 8, 2008, http://online.wsj.com/article/SB122610420534009957.html.

25. Charles Krauthammer, "Obama, the Mortal," *Washington Post*, September 4, 2009, www.washingtonpost.com/wp-dyn/content/article/2009/09/03/AR2009090302859.html.

Acknowledgments

I'm lucky to count thousands of people on my "free list" at JasonKelly.com. They send me their stories, their reactions to current events, and material that makes my books better. They're faster than the media at finding the truth of the moment. To all of them I extend a hearty thank you, and to the following members whose stories appear in this book, a special nod of gratitude: Carlos Cao, Jack Chism, Andrew Crawford, Bud Garofalo, Darin Grant, Richard Grant, Tom Hohmeier, Lee Kilgore, Charles Kirk, Neal Lonky, Laura Reynold, Aaron Sweyne, and Sarp Yeletaysi.

If you're not already on the list, join us. It takes just a moment to enter your e-mail address, and I promise not to send you any credit card ads.

Thanks to my editing team at John Wiley & Sons: Debra Englander, Kelly O'Connor, Adrianna Johnson, and Claire Wesley. They embraced the book's title and saw its potential to get across a message that's been mostly lost in the financial fray. Our world needs more bold people like them.

Finally, thanks to my old buddy and financial writing whiz, Dan Denning, for loving the concept of the book and putting me in touch with Debra at John Wiley & Sons.

About the Author

Jason Kelly is the author of eight books, including *The Neatest Little Guide to Stock Market Investing*, a *BusinessWeek* best seller. He writes financial and political articles at JasonKelly .com, keeps in touch with readers on the site's free e-mail list, and provides investment commentary to subscribers of *The Kelly Letter*. He graduated in 1993 from the University of Colorado at Boulder with a Bachelor of Arts in English. He currently lives in Sano, Japan, north of Tokyo.

Index

Index

Index

Index

Index

Index

Index

Index

Index